The Reminiscences

of

Rear Admiral Frederic Stanton Withington,

U. S. Navy (Retired)

U. S. Naval Institute
Annapolis, Maryland
1972

Preface

This manuscript is the result of a series of tape recorded interviews with Rear Admiral Frederic S. Withington, U. S. Navy (Retired). The interviews were obtained by John T. Mason, Jr., under the aegis of the Oral History program of the U. S. Naval Institute, Annapolis, Maryland. The interviews were all held during the month of June, 1971 in the home of Admiral Withington in Washington, D. C.

Admiral Withington has seen the transcript of the recordings and has made a number of minor corrections and emendations. The reader is reminded that the transcript is a record of the spoken word rather than the written word.

An index is added in the thought that it will prove useful to the researcher who uses the manuscript.

DECLARATION OF TRUST

The undersigned does hereby appoint and designate as his ~~(my)~~ Trustee herein, the Secretary-Treasurer and Publisher of the United States Naval Institute to perform and discharge the following duties, powers, and privileges in connection with the possession and use of a certain taped interview between the undersigned and the Oral History Department of the United States Naval Institute.

1. Classification of Transcript.

(✓)a. If classified OPEN, the transcript(s) may be read or the recording(s) audited by the qualified personnel upon presentation of proper credentials, as determined by the Secretary-Treasurer of the U. S. Naval Institute.

( )b. If classified PERMISSION REQUIRED TO CITE OR QUOTE, the user will be required to obtain permission in writing from the interviewee prior to quoting or citing from either the transcript(s) or the recording(s).

( )c. If classified PERMISSION REQUIRED, permission must be obtained in writing from the interviewee before the transcribed interview(s) can be examined or the tape recording(s) audited.

( )d. If classified CLOSED, the transcribed interview(s) and the tape recording(s) will be sealed until a time specified by the interviewee. This may be until the death of the interviewee or for any specified number of years.

2. It is expressly understood that in giving this authorization, I am in no way precluded from placing such restrictions as I may desire upon use of the interview at any time during my lifetime, nor does this authorization in any way affect my rights to the copyright of my literary expressions that may be contained in the interview.

Witness my hand and seal this 20th day of September 1971.

Frederic S. Withington

I hereby accept and consent to the foregoing Declaration of Trust and the powers therein conferred upon me as Trustee:

R. E. Bowker Jr.

REAR ADMIRAL FREDERIC S. WITHINGTON, U. S. NAVY, RETIRED

Frederic Stanton Withington was born in Rutherford, New Jersey, on November 1, 1901. He attended West High School, Des Moines, Iowa, before his appointment as Midshipman to the U. S. Naval Academy from the Seventh District of Iowa in 1919. As a First Classman, he was editor of the "Lucky Bag." Graduated and commissioned Ensign in June 1923, he subsequently attained the rank of Captain to date from May 1, 1943. His selection for the rank of Rear Admiral, approved by the President on December 29, 1949, was confirmed by the Senate to date from May 1, 1950.

After graduation in June 1923, he had brief duty in the Bureau of Ordnance, Navy Department, Washington, D. C., and from August to November of that year was under instruction in torpedoes at the Naval Torpedo Station, Newport, Rhode Island. He assisted in fitting out the USS WEST VIRGINIA, and served in that battleship from her commissioning, December 1, 1923, until June 1928. Three succeeding years he was under instruction in Ordnance Engineering at the Postgraduate School, Annapolis, Maryland, and the Navy Yard, Washington, D. C. He served in the USS NEVADA from June 1931 until May 1934, after which he had a tour of duty at the Naval Gun Factory, Navy Yard, Washington, D. C.

In June 1936 he reported for duty as Aide and Flag Lieutenant on the Staff of Commander, Battleship Division 3, Battle Fleet, USS WEST VIRGINIA, flagship, continuing Staff duty from June 1937 until June 1938 in the USS CHICAGO, flagship of Commander Crusiers, Scouting Force, U. S. Fleet. After a year's service in the USS WINSLOW, he had duty from June 1939 until March 1942 in the Bureau of Ordnance, Navy Department, Washington, D. C., serving first in the Fire Control Section, and later in the Production Division. For meritorious service in that assignment, he received a Letter of Commendation, with Ribbon, from the Secretary of the Navy.

Assigned duty in connection with fitting out the USS INDIANA, he joined that ship when she was commissioned April 30, 1942, and served from May 1942 until November 1943 as her Gunnery Officer, and until October 1944 as her Executive Officer. During his service aboard the INDIANA, assigned to the South Pacific Fleet, operated in the Southern Solomons during January 1943, and participated in the New Georgia Campaign beginning in June of that year. Transferred to the Central Pacific in August 1943, she participated with a carrier group in the air strikes against Marcus Island, in the occupation of the Gilbert Islands, and in the bombardment of Nauru.

He received a Letter of Commendation with authorization to wear the star on his Commendation Ribbon, from the Commender in Chief, Pacific Fleet, for meritorious service as Gunnery and Executive Officer of the USS INDIANA from April 1942 to June 1944. Immediately thereafter he became Chief of Staff and Aide to the Commander Group TWO, Fifth Amphibious

Force, operating in the Central Pacific areas. For "exceptionally merituous conduct in the performance of outstanding service from January 1944 to October 1944..." in the coordination of "detailed study and planning of each operation, displaying exceptional ability and untiring devotion to duty..." he was awarded the Legion of Merit.

On November 28, 1944 he reported for duty in the Bureau of Ordnance, Navy Department, Washington, D. C. In October of the following year, he was assigned as Officer in Charge of the Naval Ordnance Laboratory, Navy Yard, Washington, D. C. He was ordered detached in January 1947, and thereafter until August 1948 served in successive command of the USS MISSISSIPPI, and the USS MANCHESTER. Completing the course at the National War College, Washington, D. C., in June 1949, he reported in July to the Office of the Chief of Naval Operations, Navy Department, where he served first as Assistant Director of the Atomic Energy Division, and from January 1951 as Director.

He was Commander Amphibious Group THREE from November 1952 to December 1953, when he reported as Deputy and Assistant Chief of the Bureau of Ordnance, Navy Department. On November 16, 1954 he was nominated to be Chief of the Bureau of Ordnance, for a term of four years, his nomination confirmed by the Senate, December 2, 1954. In April 1958 he became Commander Naval Forces, Japan, and for "exceptionally meritorious conduct...(in that capacity) from April 1958 to April 1961..." he was awarded a Gold Star in lieu of the Second Legion of Merit. The citation further states in part:

"An inspiring leader and diplomat, Rear Admiral Withington has been eminently successful in implementing the spirit of the President's People-to-People Program throughout his command, resulting in the strengthening and furtherance of cooperation and friendship between United States naval personnel and the Japanese people. Through his active interest in and assistance to the Japanese Maritime Self Defense Force, he has contributed materially to the high degree of readiness of that Force, and has brought about closer cooperation between our two navies at all levels. Rear Admiral Withington has insisted that 'service to the fleet' be more than just a motto in the Japanese ports under his control, thereby making a significant contribution to the efficiency and readiness of the SEVENTH Fleet. In dealing with high-ranking Japanese government and military officials, he has consistently exercised a high degree of professional skill and diplomacy..."

Rear Admiral Withington was transferred to the Retired List of the U. S. Navy on April 1, 1961.

In addition to the Legion of Merit with Gold Star and the Commendation Ribbon with star, Rear Admiral Withington has the American Defense Service Medal; American Campaign Medal; Asiatic-Pacific Campaign Medal; World War II Victory Medal; Navy Occupation Service Medal, Europe Clasp;

R. Adm. R. S. Withington, USN, Ret.   Page 3

National Defense Service Medal; Korean Service Medal; and the United Nations Service Medal. He also has the following foreign awards: Order of Naval Merit by Brazil, Order of Crown (Cross of Commander) by Belgium and the Honorary Officer in the Order of the British Empire by Great Britain.

His official home address is 5141 Palisade Lane, N. W., Washington, D. C. He is married to the former Louise F. Gleason of New York, New York.

Navy Office of Information
Internal Relations Division (OI-430)
21 April 1961

Interview No. 1 with Rear Admiral Frederick S. Withington, U. S. Navy, (Retired)

Place: His residence in Washington, D. C.

Date: Monday morning, 7 June 1971

Subject: Biography

By: John T. Mason, Jr.

Q: It's certainly nice to meet you, Admiral. I've been looking forward to this series. Admiral Hooper told me something about you, and Admiral Waters did also the other day. So I am most anxious to hear your account of your distinguished naval career.

Would you begin, Sir, in the proper way by telling me the date and place of your birth, and then something about your family background?

Adm. W.: I was born on the 1st of November 1901 in Rutherford, New Jersey. My father was a life insurance actuary who worked for many years for the Mutual Life Insurance Company in New York City. My mother had been a school teacher, and was twenty years younger than he. There were two other children in the family, a younger brother and a younger sister. Shortly after my birth, the family moved to Des Moines, Iowa, where my father became an independent consulting actuary.

Q: What induced him to go West?

Adm. W.: He wished to be independent, and he was reasonably successful at this. We had quite a series of ups and downs in his long life. After some years in Iowa, we moved to California where he was employed by the California Western States Life Insurance

Company, and the family lived in Berkeley. Berkeley in those days was a halcyon place with a budding, but rather small, school called the University of California - and no riots. I rode a bicycle with great pleasure, delivered newspapers, alike on the bicyle and on roller skates, and enjoyed the town exceedingly.

During our period of residence in California, the Exposition at San Francisco took place and this was one of my early pleasant memories. I remember particularly seeing Beachy fly an airplane, and this was quite a sight in 1914.

Q: It certainly was!

Adm. W.: We moved again - we returned, rather, to Iowa from California in 1914 and we lived there during most of my time in high school.

Q: Where was this, Iowa City?

Adm. W.: Des Moines, again. I did reasonably well in high school and had an opportunity shortly after graduation to aspire to the Naval Academy. Iowa is a long way from the sea, but I happened to see a Lucky Bag, which is the annual of the Naval Academy, and I was seduced by all these beautiful young men and their pictures in this beautifully bound book.

Q: How did your family react to the idea of the Naval Academy?

Adm. W.: They were very pleased. I was entered in a local college but there was very little money in the till and it was very convenient that I was able to go to the Naval Academy where money was not required.

Withington #1 - 3

Q: They didn't object to it? Your mother didn't object to a military career?

Adm. W.: No. I was fortunate in being able to get a principal appointment and worked entirely at home, working on the basis of using former examinations, studying them, and working out the answers to the problems, and I passed with exceedingly high marks. I was the only one of Congressman Dowell's candidates to pass that year - Cassius C. Dowell. Parenthetically, some time not too long after graduation, I called upon my congressman, as one is supposed to do, in Washington. The subject was a proposal then to increase officers' pay, and Mr. Dowell looked at me over his glasses and said, "Son, if you had the money you'd spend it, wouldn't you?" and that was the end of the interview. There was no pay raise at that time.

Q: Tell me, Admiral, how much time did you spent at Drake University?

Adm. W.: I never went there at all.

Q: Oh, you didn't go there at all?

Adm. W.: The appointment came through before.

Q: If you had gone to Drake, what had you anticipated studying?

Adm. W.: I had very fuzzy ideas about what I should like. Really, none.. My age then was sixteen and one is hardly mature at that time of life.

Q: Very few young men at that age have a definite objective.

Adm. W.: Yes.

Q: So, you went to the Naval Academy on a principal appointment?

Adm. W.: Yes. This was my first time away from home and I thought for the first two or three weeks I was going to die from homesickness, especially when they played "Taps" at ten o'clock at night in Bancroft Hall, but I survived.

Q: Did your Dad accompany you out east?

Adm. W.: Oh, no, I came on my own. In those days, the midshipmen were very much secluded. In fact, we were in a quasi prisoner status. The plebes were almost never allowed out in town for any reason whatever. There were no weekend leaves for plebes. Midshipmen, including first class men, were not allowed even to ride in automobiles. Of course, automobiles in the period 1919 to 1923 were not very plentiful, anyhow. So I survived, and all my classmates, the rigors of plebe year and plebe summer. In those days there was a considerable amount of physical hazing as well as mental hazing, which has now, I think properly, been abolished - the physical side has been abolished. I was a terrible little prig when I went there at the age of seventeen years and eight months, and I got hell beaten out of me for it for a year, and I think I lost it all. I have no regrets.

Q: Then it served you well.

Adm. W.: Yes, it did.

Q: Why? Because of your abilities at your studies? Is that why you felt that you were a prig?

Withington #1 - 5

Adm. W.: No. I think it was more or less the fault of my father and my mother. My father was born in Boston in 1859. He didn't marry till he was forty. My mother was of Quaker extraction and she was born in Philadelphia. My father was a genealogist and a good one, and he had printed through the New England Genealogical Society a story of the Withington family. My mother's ancestry goes back a long way also, and he worked that out. Unfortunately, this genealogy appeared about 1930 and no one in the Withington family has had the interest or the ability to bring it up to date. Of course, there would be many more names. Since I have two children and six grandchildren, I'm only just one member and there are many other members.

Q: Maybe that's a task before you in retirement!

Adm. W.: Yes. The original Withington was a blacksmith who came from central south England. In fact, there is a town there still called Withington. The name, oddly enough, has roots in the old Saxon word for taxes, which is wythe. This is not considered with a great deal of pleasure, but I believe it to be true.

My plebe year was reasonably successful. I did well in studies, and we went on the first summer cruise in some of the old battleships that had gone round the world in 1908. These ships were very tired and the worst feature of all of them, I think, was the fact that the evaporators, the machines that made fresh water from the sea, were exceedingly poor. The water was brackish and very inadequate. Our allowance was half a bucket per day for midshipmen or for sailors in the crew. The crew was the leavings from World War I, and the ships would not have moved except for the midshipmen, who did the work of firing the boilers and passing the coal.

Q: They were old coal-burners, were they?

Adm. W.: Oh, they were all old coal-burners. The ventilation in the fire room spaces was entirely inadequate, and as a result, within a week, the midshipmen dropped more or less like flies. They were hauled up on deck and revived by having the salt-water hose turned on them. However, we all survived this and somehow or other we made the ships move, including one long leg of several thousand miles direct from Panama to Hawaii. This was good experience for all of us young fellows and, as I say, we all survived it with the help of the salt-water hose.

Q: That was the summer...

Adm. W.: The summer of 1920.

Q: To Hawaii and back?

Adm. W.: Yes. We came down the West coast from Seattle to San Francisco to Los Angeles. It was a long, long voyage and, considering all the ships, produced many thousands of tons of ashes from the coal we burned. None of us will ever forget the difficulty of getting clean after coaling ship.

Q: With so little water!

Adm. W.: Yes.

Q: Were any of you discouraged at the prospect of becoming naval officers, as a result of this experience?

Withington #1 - 7

Adm. W.: I think not. I don't believe anybody was motivated to leave the Naval Academy because of the rigors of the cruise. A good many young boys, including my room mate, resigned voluntarily because they did not think that a future in the Navy appealed to them. My room mate thought he could study law at the Naval Academy; that happened to others also. Others failed academically. This was, of course, and is still, the largest reason for the attrition at the Naval Academy. We entered 720 strong and graduated 412. Our attrition was roughly 40 percent, which was then normal and is still more or less the experience, I believe. It's pretty rough but in any system where quality is stressed, selectivity is necessary and you can't have any other result.

Q: And considering the different levels of high-school preparation, this is natural.

Adm. W.: Many of the boys then, and I think also now, spent a period of some months, perhaps as much as a year, in a special preparatory school, and this is helpful. Some of the older midshipmen then, and more of them now, I believe, have had a year or possibly two years at college before going to Annapolis, and this is exceedingly helpful in the present state at Annapolis when the educational opportunities are much extended and it's possible to major in, say, Russian. I'm not sure that all this is a good idea, but it certainly has kept the Naval Academy up to date, and this is a good thing I believe on the whole, also at West Point and the Air Force Academy.

Q: I understand from various men that in those earlier years if they did have a year in college beforehand, then the first year at the Naval Academy was fairly boring because it was just a repetition ...

Adm. W.: This was true in my day. It's not true now because you can validate the subject which you have already studied, and presumably, hopefully, have time to go on to other fields of interest. The first time, really, out of the stockade, so to speak, was September leave after the youngster cruise. I went home and ordered my uniform, and generally swashbuckled and swished around the town.

Q: That was real compensation!

Adm. W.: That was some compensation, yes. Youngster year we took calculus, and I fortunately was able to develop a facility for it, and I undertook to teach it to some of my more unhappy classmates who were having great difficulty in passing. I had a class after study hours every evening at 9:30 for most of that year. This was not entirely altruism because it enabled me to understand the subject a lot better than I otherwise would have, but as a result of this effort I became rather well known in the class, and they elected me to be the editor of the <u>Lucky Bag</u>. This is the annual of the Naval Academy, and it's always been a very distinguished publication in which a great deal of effort and money has been invested. This one was one of the last, I believe, to be bound in actual leather. They use fabricord now, and it's much more sensible because the leather may have cost us $10,000 I'm not sure, but it was a lot. The whole effect, moneywise, was worth some $40,000, and the business manager had to sweat blood to sell enough copies to pay for all this, but we did sell them and we did make a considerable profit. And we won the prize that year for producing the best college annual.

Q: You must have shown some literary ability before you were named to this job, too, didn't you?

Adm. W.: The authorities had nothing to do with the selection of the editor of the Lucky Bag. I did do well in English at the Naval Academy and I still consider it to be the most important subject taught there or at any college. If a man can't communicate, he is really not competent to be a leader of other men or indeed to be a first classman in any line of endeavor, I think. This is a deeply felt belief.

Q: And the concurrent ability to speak in public. Did you have any training in that area?

Adm. W.: We were not as well trained as the midshipmen are, I understand, today. We were required once a year, to have an after-dinner speech session in the basement of Bancroft Hall in groups of about twenty with an instructor, and this was considered to be extra duty and torture by all hands. Of course, it was good for us and we didn't have enough of it. We did have a head of department, C. Alphonso Smith, in English, who was the greatest teacher in my experience, and I have him to thank for whatever fluency I may have in my native language, and I think all of my classmates feel the same way about him. He's long gone to his reward. His son used to be the tennis champion of the Navy for many years. He became a naval officer.

Q: Did you have any special activities in athletics? Were you

Withington #1 - 10

interested?

Adm. W.: My only athletic effort was involved in getting off the so-called Submarine Squad. I was a very poor swimmer, and still am, and for two of my four years at Annapolis I had to go to extra instruction sessions at the swimming pool. A willing classmate almost allowed himself to be drowned while I "saved" him and towed him across the pool and delivered him to the other side still aliv but by a very narrow margin. No, my ability as an athlete was meager, to say the least. There was not as much pressure in our day as there is now on the midshipmen to do something athletically I think maybe there wasn't enough pressure. I was strictly an arm chair athlete, and this Lucky Bag business required many, many of my hours, including time after taps.

Actually, the Lucky Bag took so many hours that I would not have been able to do anything significant in any other line. But I never regretted it. I learned a great deal from the experience.

Q: You had to be an exceptionally good student to carry that extra load, didn't you?

Adm. W.: I did well in studies. I starred in two of the four years, and graduated 20 in a class of 412.

Q: Tell me about the other summer cruises.

Adm. W.: We were fortunate the second-class cruise was to Europe, to Christiania, which is now Oslo, in Norway, and we went to Lisbo where we saw the bull fights where the bulls are not killed, which

PORTUGAL

I'm glad to say is still the case in ~~Lisbon~~. This European cruise was very pleasant for us all. My amount of money available was quite meager, ~~but~~ I remember vividly in Christiania scrubbing my classmates' hammocks for 25 cents a hammock in order to make a few dollars. Our pay was very small in those days, and the amount of cash the midshipmen were allowed was on the order of, maybe, two dollars a month for plebes and ten dollars a month for first classmen. The situation is now entirely different. I'm not sure whether it's better or not! But we knew the value of money in our day and I'm not sure that the current generation of midshipmen know it as well as we did.

Our first-class cruise was to the Caribbean and to Halifax, and this included shooting target practice off Guantanamo, which was good for us. We learned a lot by our mistakes and that's what the idea was. All the midshipmen made all the cruises in our day. Now this is no longer the case. The ships are not available. It's too expensive to keep obsolescent ships in commission for that purpose alone. It can't be done. As you know, the Navy has contracted by some 200 ships in the last year. So the midshipmen are parceled out in small numbers to active-fleet ships, and there is one summer, I believe, when the second class gets flight training somewhere. Then there's part of one summer when they view an amphibious exercise at Little Creek. They don't get as good background in the sea as we did. There isn't any comparison, and I think this is a pity.

Q: I suppose that was only possible because they used the battleships?

Adm. W.: The old ships were available and they didn't cost much to keep up. They were small and the fuel consumption was low, the crews were small in numbers. They maintained a bare skeleton crew when the midshipmen came aboard for the summer cruises. That's all gone, and it's too bad.

Q: I would think that the summer cruises, especially as you progressed toward graduation, would be a way of putting into practice some of the theories that you had learned.

Adm. W.: We were all required to navigate, and taking your own star sights and sun sights was quite different from the so-called P-works which you had to do at Annapolis. We were required to stand deck watch and, of course, we were the firemen and coal passers down in the engineering spaces, we stood the engine room watches. We learned by doing, and this is the only way you ever get there. To a considerable extent this is true now, but in our day the ship went or stopped depending upon whether the midshipmen produced, and this, of course, is no longer the case on any ship. They're just a little bit of extra duty for the captain and the executive officer and the division officers concerned.

Q: Did you have a brush with aviation during one of these summers?

Adm. W.: Never, no. I had a chance after graduation to go in to aviation and decided I didn't want to drive an airplane, so they put me down as temperamentally unqualified and physically able. I could see in those days. I didn't need glasses.

Q: "Temperamentally unqualified" because you didn't want to!

Adm. W.: Yes. A good many of my classmates did go into aviation

Withington #1 - 13

and were very successful.

Q: In reflection, what would you say about the course of study in your day?

Adm. W.: It was entirely too restricted. There was no choice whatever, except that between French and Spanish as a language. We all took the same curriculum, completely the same, regardless of whether we'd had a couple of years of college or were struggling to make two fives, a passing mark. I think that certainly the changes toward widening the opportunities, the educational opportunities, are for the better.

Q: What about the caliber of the teaching staff?

Adm. W.: There was a very much higher percentage of officer instructors in our day than there is today. The caliber of their education was not as high and definitely the quality of teaching, I think, was not as good. We were more or less required to man the boards when we went to the classrooms. We were required to have a mark every day, and the instructor was the referee rather than the teacher in many, many cases. You learned yourself or you didn't learn, this method undoubtedly has real advantages but it had disadvantages, too.

Q: And there was much learning by rote, was there not?

Adm. W.: Yes, especially in ordnance and gunnery. We were required to solve problems which required massive use of logarithm tables, and this was not very useful in the learning process. After you looked up one logarithm, you looked up them all. I don't wish to give the impression that our education was inferior, because it was a good education. I have already mentioned that I was particularly happy with the English course and did exceedingly well. That was the only time I ever stood one in a month in anything there - that would be one month in English.

I might say a word about the discipline. It was, of course, of two types. The discipline administered by the midshipmen themselves, which largely in my day consisted of hazing the plebes ...

Q: That was fairly severe, wasn't it?

Adm. W.: That was fairly severe. There was not as much participation by the midshipmen, especially the first classmen, in the control of the discipline of the brigade as there is today, and this is a great change for the better, in my opinion. There was then and there is now a so-called grease mark, an efficiency report mark on every midshipmen, and this is more properly called "aptitude for the service." But the grease mark presented by the midshipmen was perhaps, more graphic and in some cases more precise because there were some midshipmen who were definitely greasing. They were lick spittles when an officer was in sight, and they were not the best possible prospects for naval officers, in my opinion, then or now.

Life in Bancroft Hall was, I think, essentially the same then as it is now. We had a minor insurrection in my youngster year, which was a flare-up about hazing, and it was sufficiently serious so that the superintendent put in a policy of segregation. He put the plebes off by themselves in Bancroft Hall, apart from the upperclassmen. This was not a very popular move on the part of the upper-class men. The plebe class was the class of 1924, and this segregation lasted for a long time - too long, I think. The relationship between the class of 1924 and the three older classes were never very happy thereafter, and it was most unfortunate all around.

The insurrection was of such magnitude that the midshipmen were throwing things out of the windows of the inner courtyard, throwing burning rolls of toilet paper, and the superintendent and the commandant thought that something had to be done.

Q: Something drastic!

Adm. W.: Something drastic. But I'm not sure that the actual complete segregation of the plebe class from the upper classes was a good move.

Q: That must have been awfully difficult to achieve, anyway.

Adm. W.: Everybody had to move, and to make matters worse, they moved the plebes into the new wing, which was the most attractive and pleasant for living purposes. It was not a good time, a very sad time, in the history of the Naval Academy.

Q: What was the incident that touched this off?

Adm. W.: The brutal beating of a couple of midshipmen, but I'm not quite sure that I remember. It was necessary to expel two or three upper-class men. I don't think there was a death involved. There was one death in our time at the Naval Academy. One poor kid, in my class I think, went crazy over the subject of English, oddly enough, and jumped to his death from a fourth-floor window into the moat at Bancroft Hall. He was physically and mentally quite unqualified to be a midshipman. Of course, this is bound to happen. An occasional misfit will get through. He usually just quietly departs after failing, he doesn't take things into his own hands and take his own life, as that one did. This death cast a pall over the - it was the regiment, then, and not the brigade - for a long, long time.

It was in general a more monastic life than it is now for the midshipmen, a more restricted life, but it was a very good one, and I'm not sure that possibly the incessant concern with the Navy wasn't better for molding future naval officers than the present more permissive life. I don't know. I do know that many of the products of the ROTC system certainly are becoming senior officers and flag officers, and this seems to work, and of course nothing could be more dissimilar to the Naval Academy of my day than the ROTC system of today -

I don't believe I have anything more of interest to add to the Naval Academy time. Admiral Henry B. Wilson was superintendent and he was a swashbuckling, handsome man, who always wore his cap on the side of his head and was really a great inspiration to the midshipmen. He never did much of anything. He let the commandant do all the dirty work, but this is the way to run the Naval Academy and I hope they still do it that way.

Q: After you graduated you had a most unusual short duty in the Bureau of Ordnance.

Adm. W.: This happened for a very simple reason. I was ordered with a large group of about thirty of my classmates to the West

Virginia, which was the new battleship not yet finished, so for six months they had to do something with these thirty young men, and we were strewn all over the Atlantic coast more or less between the Naval Gun Factory, the Naval Torpedo Station at Newport, the Bureau of Ordnance, the Naval Powder Factory at Indian Head, and the Naval Proving Ground at Dahlgren, Virginia. I believe that was all of our destinations.

We were very much in the way wherever we went, but we did learn something here and there, I guess.

Q: Is this what induced you to direct your future efforts in this area?

Adm. W.: I think that may be so, yes. These were all interesting places and they were handy for the East Coast. The ship was being built at Newport News, and there wasn't much money in those days for the Navy, and specially for Navy travel, and it didn't cost much to ship us from one place to another on the East Coast where our ship was being built.

I didn't actually report for my first duty on the West Virginia until the 1st of December 1923.

Q: In the meantime you had been at...

Adm. W.: All these other places.

Q: What field did you especially...?

Adm. W.: I think that the sense of freedom from the walls was the thing that appealed to us most; that first summer especially. Not nearly as many of us got married at graduation as happens now. I wasn't married for three years. I had found the girl by the time graduation came, but her father wisely decided that we were not to marry until I had served my three years as an ensign and had graduated from $143 a month to $271 a month - I believe those numbers are right. They're quite small compared to the pay of a junior officer today, but as far as what can be bought with the money, about the same, I would say.

Q: I suppose today with the greater freedom at the Academy the boys have a better chance to select a future wife than you did?

Adm. W.: That's right. The tendency of those who did marry at graduation was to marry the girl from back home, and some of these marriages didn't work out well at all and failed sooner or later because the girl was entirely unable to cope with Navy life.

Q: And had no concept of it!

Adm. W.: No. She came to Annapolis from Podunk somewhere and was wrapped up in the assembly line of a Naval Academy chapel wedding - there was an assembly line even in those days, not anything like as bad as it is now - and here she was in the Navy with $183 a month to live on, including her husband's rental allowance of $40. And this was not easy, especially if she got pregnant right away.

I was on the West Virginia almost five years with time out for a year's staff duty, and this was too long in one ship. Most of my classmates had long since gone on to the Asiatic Station or to destroyers and they got a broader preparation for the Navy than I did.

Q: Why did you stay that long?

Withington #1 - 19

Adm. W.: I didn't have much choice. I was not ordered elsewhere. I didn't make any great attempt to go elsewhere. I think in retrospect this was a mistake.

Q: Did this mean that you had shown real ability in whatever you were assigned in on the battleship and therefore they wanted to keep you there?

Adm. W.: Presumably, they had a retention list, yes. I know they did, as a matter of fact.

Q: What were your particular duties?

Adm. W.: Mostly deck duties. I had only one tour of engineering duty in later years, one year in a later battleship. And this again was a little bit warping. I didn't really get as much rounded duty as would have been otherwise desirable. My staff duty was as a young staff communicator, as an ensign, and this was broadening. I learned how the wheels went around in the Navy by reading all the messages, because this was my duty, it wasn't snooping. I remember especially one message. The fleet had been on a cruise to Panama and on the return many private messages were going ashore for delivery to the wives, and this one boy's message said, "Arriving Sunday morning, 0800 Long Beach. Don't get up."! I know he said it because I saw it and transmitted it for him.

Q: Did you have a good set of officers in the West Virginia?

Adm. W.: We had a very happy ship. One of my captains was Watt Tyler Cluverius, who has now gone but was a very distinguished naval officer. I remember particularly his kindness to me when our first child was born. I duly reported back to the ship having assisted as far as possible at the launching. The captain sent for me and I didn't understand what this might be about. When the orderly announced me in his cabin, he looked over his glasses at me from his desk, and said, "How was the princess this morning?" I've never forgotten his comment. A really kindly thing to do to a young and harassed father!

Q: Well, the right officers for this first cruise really make a great difference, don't they?

Adm. W.— Yes. This was one of the newest ships in the Navy. The Navy was quite small in those days, as you know. The appropriation for one year was something like $350,000,000. It was a very unbalanced Navy with destroyers and battleships, very few cruisers very inadequate in design. The aircraft carrier Langley was, of course, the first carrier. Then, for years, the Lexington and the Saratoga were the only two carriers in the Navy. Only in the late 1930s did the Navy really develop effective carriers of the type of the Enterprise.

Q: In the immediate postwar period, the future of the Navy was not very great, was it?

Adm. W.: No, it was very much in doubt.

Q: That was a war to end all wars. Was there any inclination on the part of your classmates to leave the service?

Adm. W.: There were quite a few departures. I think relatively fewer then than there are today. The Depression had quite a bit to do with this. Not during my first cruise on the West Virginia, but my second cruise on the battleship Nevada the Navy was one of the few activities in the United States where you were assured of the next pay check and three square meals. We had to take a 15 percent pay cut which didn't help our morale any, but at least we could still eat. Indeed, for a period there in Long Beach the Navy checks were the only checks which were being accepted in the local banks. This was the time of the Bank Holiday in 1933.

Q: Today, you hear so much about the family pull on the young officer to leave the service and establish himself in some business where there's a permanent residence. Was there any of that in those days? How did the wives react to a Navy career, did they go along with it willingly?

Adm. W.: I know the situation was quite different. We used to think that our separations were very difficult to bear, but actually they were seldom longer than three months. Now, when on deployment to the Mediterranean or the Far East, it's nine months and may be, regretably, much longer. I think the life on the young wives today is much harder than it was on our wives in my day. I know it. And this is one of the ~~great~~ reasons for the great attrition of junior officers and the catastrophic drop in the re-enlistment rate in the Navy today. We're terribly over-extended relative to my day, with commitments all around the world.

Q: The experience of commissioning a battleship must have been an interesting one, and also one from which you could learn a great deal.

Adm. W.: Yes. I saw it from the worm's eye view as an ensign, and then later as a senior lieutenant commander in the battleship Indiana during World War II. It's a very difficult time bringing a large chunk of iron to life. It was easier in West Virginia days than it was in the days of World War II because there were many more professional officers then. The Navy was small. The quality of men available as petty officers was high, relatively, and young men were pretty generally well educated.

The organization of a ship is pretty well standardized by the type commander today, and it was in those days also, but there was a great deal of room for individual thought and effort, details of how things were going to be done on board ship. If these were well planned and well done, the ship got off to a good start. We did in the West Virginia. Other ships did not.

Q: You weren't under great pressure either, timewise, were you?

Adm. W.: No. There wasn't any such thing as a deployment. In those days there wasn't any fleet in the Mediterranean. Usually we had an old cruiser. For years she was the Pittsburgh. She was the ship on the European Station, and that was it. We didn't have the treaty commitments then that we have now, and these are what are killing the military. We're so drastically overcommitted relative to the force we actually have available.

Q: Would you say a little about the shakedown cruise of the West Virginia?

Adm. W.: Yes. This was a very sad occasion really. We left Hampton Roads, and right in the middle of the 40-foot channel we ran aground on the way to France and England. This was not very good. We filled the condensers with mud and had to be ignominiously ~~be~~ towed back to the Navy yard to have the condensers cleaned out before we could proceed. The navigator, of course, was not hung for this, being in the channel at the time, but it was a rather bad way to start a new ship.

Q: Was there a board...?

Adm. W.: Oh, yes. But it was quite obvious that we were in the channel, clear to everybody concerned These ships drew about 36 feet, loaded, and the channel was supposed to be 40, and it wasn't at that point, and we were heavily loaded with fuel oil for the cruise.

We got off all right, and met our commitments in France and England. I spent all my money in Paris, ~~I had~~ very little, having $300 in graduation debts still to be paid, and that was a lot of money in those days. So when we got to the Channel coast of England, I was unable financially to go to London which was a great cross to bear, but I couldn't do it. During this period of shakedown I was wooing by mail the lady who is now my wife. This was Louise Gleason of New York City, whose father and mother both came from Montpelier, Vermont. He was a successful corporation lawyer in New York City. I met her on a blind date at the Naval Academy when I was a first classman. It all started then and I've been very happy about it ever since.

We were married in 1926 ~~at the family home~~ in East Hampton, Long Island. Most of the ushers were young naval officers then attending the submarine school in New London, across the Sound.

Unfortunately, the very evening before the wedding ~~was~~, the hostess who put most of them up at her house had liquor available in great quantity in their rooms, although this was Prohibition days, and by the time the bachelor dinner was over and we were supposed to meet the bridesmaids for a joint ~~dinner~~ PARTY, most of the ushers including the bridegroom-to-be were definitely inebriated, and the combined party was a dismal failure! In fact, the debacle was a source of some comment for a long time thereafter among the people of East Hampton. However, the wedding came off, as planned, the next afternoon in spite of a thunderstorm that caused the power to fail, and all went well.

Q: Going back to the West Virginia and the shakedown cruise, what - tell me a little bit about damage control on a battleship at that time.

Adm. W.: There was almost none. There were, of course, watertight doors and the ship was divided into watertight compartments, but there wasn't any damage-control officer so called, he was called the first lieutenant, and he was more or less the janitor who kept the ship clean. Had we had a proper damage-control organization which never did really come into effect in the Navy until we learned the hard way in World War II, we might have done better in the grounding, but I doubt it. The intakes to the condensers which were clogged with mud were on the bottom of the ship, and we didn't know we were going aground, obviously! But had we closed the intakes, the whole engineering plant would have gone up in smoke ~~more or less~~ without any cooling water. But, to answer your question there was essentially no damage control representation at all.

Q: Did you carry a plane?

Adm. W.: Not on our shakedown cruise. The planes on the battleships were developed in the later 1920s and the 1930s, and occasionally, only in one or two cases, a plane was carried on top of a high turret. Usually it was on a catapult on the stern, which was either air-or powder-operated. It was a fairly chintzy thing. I would never have wanted to be an aviator and be catapulted from a battleship or a cruiser under way. We learned how to retrieve the plane by turning across the wind and making a slick upon which the aviator would hopefully land. Occasionally he would capsize in the process. Then he would taxi up towards the stern and catch the hook underneath the pontoon into a sled which was towed from the stern. Once he was hooked, the sled was hauled in very carefully until he was underneath the crane and could be hooked on and hoisted. It was a very pretty maneuver when it was done properly, and it was done, indeed, in World War II in the battleships in the South Pacific. The pilots had to be seamen as well as pilots, and the officer in charge of the landing, usually me in the <u>Indiana</u> in later years, had to know something about the flyer's problems or else we would both be in trouble and we wouldn't get the plane and pilot back at all.

Q: They did improve the gunnery capabilities of the ship, did they not?

Adm. W.: Yes. Some of the pilots were exceedingly good at spotting for the main battery. I don't believe there was any case in World War II where the scouting from these planes achieved any results. They were very short range. They had to be light and, indeed, almost made out of bamboo to be catapulted at all. One of the planes particularly was a man-killer. Fortunately I was never on a ship that had to carry them, but there were several pilots needlessly lost because the plane was not suited at all to this kind of treatment.

The end of the battleship era for me was orders to the postgraduate school in ordnance engineering. The postgraduate school in those days was at the Naval Academy in Annapolis.

Q: The full term?

Adm. W.: Yes. It depended on your subject. I guess most of the postgraduate student officers went on to a college for their secon year, but the first year was in Annapolis. We didn't. We had two years in Annapolis, and then a third year sort of a Cook's tour of various ordnance installations - Army installations, too. We went to the Army Proving Ground at Aberdeen, and also the Chemical Warf School at Edgewood Arsenal. My family, which by that time, includ my daughter, made the rounds with me. It was a long three years. We had a nice house in Annapolis on the banks of the Severn for two years, and then on the Cook's tour the family came with me for the most part. We had a total of five months at Dahlgren, living in what amounted to a field hand's shack which had been hauled in from the woods somewhere, put on blocks, and made into "quarters." This was heated by a stove on the first floor. Hopefully a little hot air would rise from the stove through a hole in the ceiling and heat the second floor. The system didn't do very well.

Q: Really pioneering!

Adm. W.: It was not a very happy five months. My wife was pregnant and ill, and eventually had to go home. We did save the baby. It turned out to be a son. It's not fair to say that we were roughing it, because there was a commissary store and a very fine group of people living in and around the station, but our quarters were far from palatial, and that one Thanksgiving I spent all day stuffing the cracks with newspaper through which the cold air was pouring. They've since abolished this house arrangement. It's disappeared. Gone and not regretted!

The ordnance course was a good experience. I certainly found out quickly at the school how little I really knew about mathematics or anything else, as far as that's concerned. But in retrospect, I believe I had the same feeling about the course that most other postgraduates have. It was really valuable at teaching me how much I did not know, also in fostering and acquiring a certain amount of knowledge.

Q: Would you say that the course there at the Academy, PG course, was on a level with, say, MIT or some place like that?

Adm. W.: I have no means of knowing, of course, not having been to MIT. I think that as far as results were concerned we turned out as well.

Arleigh Burke, for instance, went to Michigan for chemical engineering, and, of course, for years all the naval constructors had always gone to MIT. Now from the postgraduate school in Monterey they fan out all over the country in various fields and various subjects. But in general much of the teaching at postgraduate school is still done in-house at Monterey, just as it was in my day. I think the quality of the faculty is much higher now than it was in my day, and the school is very much larger. And the same problems exist now as existed then, perhaps worse. How do you spare the best officers for two or three years from the fleet or aviation or Polaris submarines while you're educating them

Q: And they are the best ones who are selected to go to PG school are they not?

Adm. W.: They're not, I'm afraid. They can't be spared. Again this is the greater pressure that the present Navy operates under.

Q: Did you come out with a degree?

Adm. W.: Oh, I had a so-called master's degree, which doesn't mean anything to me, and it wouldn't mean anything academically, I believe, now. They're much more fussy and precise about these things now than they were in my day. We wrote more or less of a term paper, but it didn't amount to anything.

Q: On this Cook's tour, you were introduced to new types of things coming on stream. What were they?

Adm. W. There was very little. This was 1930-31. My particular job at the proving ground was to look at all the data from all the projectile impacts on armorplate and try to produce some sort of a law about what happened and what might be expected to happen in the future. It was very difficult to make any sense out of all these points on the charts, but I did the best I could at it.

Oh, yes, dive bombing was just in its infancy. In fact, the original dive bomber did his drops at Dahlgren. At one point he used a 1,000-pound water-filled bomb, and one day he had to drop deliberately off-target in order not to crash himself. This bomb landed just across the road from where my daughter and my dog were playing and sprayed them with dirt - it was that close. This was the most interesting thing in ordnance that was going on in my time at Aberdeen Proving Ground.

Q: Dive bombing?

Adm. W.: Yes. The very first attempts by the Navy to deliver bombs otherwise than by horizontal drop, and, as you know, the results were highly successful in World War II and indeed today.

Q: Was this technique being employed by other countries? Was the Royal Navy engaged in the same thing?

Adm. W.: I believe that there was some parallel effort going on in our Army Air Forces, but I'm sure that the real pioneers were our Navy pilots. And, as I say, the first work was done right there at Dahlgren. Fortunately the miss didn't eliminate my child.

The three years ashore were a long time for a young officer and I was interested in getting back to sea and in some sort of a ship other than a battleship. I was ordered briefly to a cruiser on the East Coast, and then my orders were changed to the battleship Nevada on the West Coast. Back to the drawing board! And I was there for the next three years, entirely in gunnery, although for most of one year I was made a division officer in the engineering department with additional duty in the plotting room. This was a bad compromise, I thought, but at least I learned something about engineering, which knowledge I was happy to have all through the later years of my life in the Navy.

Let me see. My daughter was born in 1928, my son was born in California in 1931. We had just arrived on the West Coast after the end of the postgraduate tour. That is the extent of our family. That sea cruise was from 1931 to 1934, and again it was all in one ship, and this was pretty confining. I didn't like it, and I tried to get ordered to a destroyer, and had no luck.

Q: Why did they keep you in gunnery?

Adm. W.: I don't know. I was just there with my nose to the grindstone.

Q: Who was the skipper of the Nevada?

Adm. W.: Captain Pye was the one I remember best. He later became an admiral and was not very successful in World War II. He is now deceased. Our gunnery officer in the Nevada was nammed Ruddock and he was quite a hero of World War II and, in fact, he is now in Annapolis graduating his youngest son, this week, and we'll see him at our house later this week here in Washington. That was the start of my friendship with a very fine man. He was the class of 1914.

Withington #1 - 31

Q: Did the Nevada stay in the Pacific the whole period?

Adm. W.: Yes. I was more or less a commuter between the East Coast and the Long Beach-San Pedro area, and this was not very broadening. In retrospect, I very much regret not having ever requested duty on the China Station. This was a great experience which will never be repeated now.

Q: Yes. All the men I've talked with will testify to that. This was terrific. And most of them as young ensigns had put in for this.

Adm. W.: It was narrowing to lead the life I did for so many years in the same type of ship. It was not proper training for command. In fact, there was no chance for a command, whereas on the China Station in gunboats you had a chance to command one of these old crocks at a relatively early age and it was good for young officers.

Well, we rusticated at Long Beach for three years from 1931 to 1934, then back to...

Q: What was the attitude in the Pacific at that time in the fleet? Japan wasn't looming yet as a potential enemy.

Adm. W.: No. During my days on the West Virginia we made a cruise in 1925, battleships only, to Australia and New Zealand, and the first day we got to Sydney the newspapers came out to the ship and on the front page, front and center, was a cartoon with a U.S. Navy battleship between Australia and the Rising Sun of Japan. They were quite aware in those days of the threat from the north, but I don't think we were, at least not at my level in the Navy.

Q: And not even in 1933 and 1934.

Adm. W.: Well, the war games always assumed that there'd be a second war and that the Japanese would be the enemy, but we didn't really believe this too strongly, I think, none of us, and that's one of the reasons for Pearl Harbor. We had a sense of security that really wasn't there at all.

Q: Was Admiral Reeves in command...?

Adm. W.: He was commander-in-chief during my day and I think while I was in the Nevada, but I'm not quite sure of that.

Q: When you were in the Pacific, did you get involved in games at Panama?

Adm. W.: Yes.

Q: The defense of Panama?

Adm. W.: Yes, we pulled off a surprise attack by planes from the Saratoga or the Lexington, I forget which, on the Canal, and we were in the force to which she was attached. This was a great feather in the cap of the commander, but I forget who it was. This was the early days of figuring what could be done with carrier aviation, and the Panama canal defenses were caught absolutely flat-footed. This was in the late 1920s.

Orders back to Washington sent me to the Navy Yard, the Gun Factory, where I was in gunnery for two years.

Q: Did this assignment please you?

Adm. W.: Yes. We had been first in Washington as part of the Cook' tour when my daughter was a baby, and we liked the setting, we were happy to have a chance to live here again. We enjoyed our two years in Washington, and I enjoyed professionally the work at the Navy Yard where I was the fire-control inspector. In those days the government itself manufactured torpedo directors and gun directors, procuring the computers - the range keepers - from the Ford Instrument Company. The optical range finders were, before the day of radar, generally from Bausch and Lomb of Rochester.

I was at this period a lieutenant, having passed through the years to promotion examinations for lieutenant, junior grade, and lieutenant. In those days the promotion examinations were a very considerable ordeal. You had to work like hell and cover enormous amounts of ground. While I was a postgraduate student I had to pass the examination to lieutenant, and this was a really very trying period for all of us who were concerned. It happened that our No. 1 man, McLaren, was in the same class with me at postgraduate school, and he and I together made out the first so-called gouge, that is, a set of answers to the expected questions, and this took many, many midnight hours. I remember this with considerable horror. We made it all right.

Q: It paid off!

Adm. W.: It paid off, yes.

Q: But promotions came very slowly.

Adm. W.: Very slowly. We were lieutenants, junior grade, after three years, and I was promoted to lieutenant after possibly eight years in the service. And lieutenant commander came about 1939, another eight years. Then, of course, the war came and all bets were off.

Q: Living must have been rather difficult, too, in the early 1930s because this was the time of the Depression with salary cuts and all the rest.

Adm. W.: Yes. During this period on the Nevada the Great Depression occurred, also the great earthquake at Long Beach took place. Our ship was in the Navy Yard, Bremerton, so I was no help to my family. The house was off its foundation and they had to get out. A classmate came by and picked up the family next morning - that same day, rather - and they all spent the night on the curb in front of his house with his wife and children. The Navy had to take charge of the town and send men ashore to prevent looting. The police had to have help. In general, public order was well maintained, but there was a great deal of damage. Fortunately, very few deaths. Most of the schools fell down. The earthquake hit at 5 p.m. when the schools were empty. It was a godsend that they weren't full of children.

By the time we got back from the Navy Yard cruise, the worst of the earthquake was over, but there was still occasional aftershocks. I was, and am, just scared and completely terrified of earthquakes. There's just nothing you can do while this giant has you in the palm of his hand.

I was surprised to receive a letter from Admiral Taussig, one of the really distinguished admirals of my day in the Navy, asking me to be his flag lieutenant. He was ordered as the battleship division commander.

Adm. W.: Never seen him. This was all done through a third party. After I indicated my willingness to accept this duty, we went to call on him and the first thing he asked, not me, but my good wife, was "when would it suit you to have me report to Long Beach!" His first thought was always - well, his children were relatively mature, but ours were small and he didn't want to discommode us any more than necessary in getting us to Long Beach. Anyway, that was the start of a very happy two-year relationship. Admiral Taussig has now gone but we still see Mrs. Taussig here in Washington.

Q: And his son is around still, Joe Taussig.

Adm. W.: Yes, his son lost his leg in World War II at Pearl Harbor, as you know. We see him occasionally.

The first years with Admiral Taussig was with the battleships. The second year he commanded all the cruisers which in those days numbered I believe sixteen, four divisions of heavy cruisers, but he was still a rear admiral. Unfortunately, he had crossed swords with Franklin Delano Roosevelt at the time he was assistant secretary of the Navy, and Admiral Taussig was right and Roosevelt was wrong, but that didn't do him any good in future years.

Q: ~~I was in that category as well, actually.~~

~~Adm. W.: Were you?~~ There was never a chance for him to be promoted beyond rear admiral. He commanded all these ships as a rear admiral. Goodness, this would never be true in today's Navy, but it was then. Captain Kent Hewett was his chief of staff, who later became admiral. We had a very distinguished group of people, and a very distinguished man to work for in Admiral Taussig. He I think accomplished a great deal in his year at that command, especially in leadership with the other division commanders and captains of the ships. We were in a war game in the Hawaiian area, I remember, during that year and he completely outclassed his opponent, surprised him, which delighted all the rest of us, naturally!

Finally, the last of my three years at sea in that cruise, in 1938-39, I went to a destroyer as executive officer at San Diego, and ~~this was my time.~~

Q: Before you tell me about that, Sir, the potential enemy was really looming up.

Adm. W.: Oh, yes, there wasn't any question about that. I don't think anybody ever thought that the Japanese would attack Pearl Harbor. We knew that they were developing aviation at just as fast a rate as we were. We did not know, of course, that their planes were of as high a quality as they actually were, especially the Zero and Betty.

Q: In your war games and in your general operations, what changes were being made in anticipation of an eventual conflict?

Adm. W.: There was a great deal more emphasis on aviation. There was sort of a budding understanding that the task group and task force would have to be developed. The first rudiments of this art were being probed at that time. Still, though, the battleships went in line ahead, majestically ploughing through the waters of the

Hawaiian Islands. I don't think the task group idea was really in effect until it was forced upon us by the war, the experience of World War II.

Q: Did we engage in any night operations?

Adm. W.: Yes, but not enough, we were not ever trained to fight the way the Japanese were.

Q: As it turned out, this was the case. I understand that we knew that they were engaging in night operations in practice, but it didn't seem to cause us to

Adm. W.: Our ordnance developments, by hindsight, were not good. Our antiaircraft at the start of World War II was not adequate. Our torpedo exploders were worthless. The torpedoes themselves were bad. I was not proud of my ordnance establishment and its accomplishments.

Q: How do you account for our lack of adequate preparation in these areas?

Adm. W.: One of the bad features was a man named Schuyler, class of 1907, who was the first engineering only duty ordnance officer in the Navy and who routinely turned down any new idea that came in to the Bureau of Ordnance from any source. This was a massive error. Why it was allowed to be done by the then chiefs of bureau I have no idea. There wasn't any real research and development outfit in the Bureau of Ordnance, per se, at that time. They had so-called type desks. There was an armor desk, projectiles desk, the powder desk, fire control desk, optical, and so on. There was no real emphasis on research and development, and this was the grave error.

Schuyler was Mr. R and D. He always said no, and we paid for it dearly, I'm afraid.

Q: When you say that there was perhaps, (even though we saw Japan looming as the potential enemy,) still we couldn't really extricate ourselves from this great long era of peace, and we were a peace-time Navy...

Adm. W.: It was very difficult really to believe that we could have a war with Japan, and while we went through the motions — I said this earlier I think — of being at war, we didn't really believe this was ever going to happen to us.

Q: We also had knowledge, I believe, of the fact that the Japanese were building landing craft of various kinds, but this seems to have had no great repercussion in the Navy Department.

Adm. W.: At my level, I was not aware of this at all. Whether Admiral Taussig was aware of the details or not I can't say. He was one of the few flag officers who took the Japanese threat seriously. He never made, as I say, high command, he hadn't got beyond rear admiral because of Mr. Roosevelt. Unfortunately, I think he had the best mind among the senior officers of his time and he was sorely missed when the war came upon us. By that time he was retired and recalled to active duty at a nominal job in the Navy Department in World War II.

Q: During your period of duty with him, did you make excursions to any of the islands in the Pacific?

Withington #1 - 39

Adm. W.: We made a very pleasant summer cruise in the cruiser Chicago through the inland passage to Alaska one summer, and this was the pleasantest part of my duty and association with him, I think. The governor of Missouri, Stark, was a Naval Academy graduate and was our guest on the cruise, and Mr. Farwell, the man who wrote The Rules of the Road from the University of Washington also went with us. The CHICAGO up to that time, 1939, was the biggest ship that had ever been through the Seymour Narrows in the Inland Passage. This is the place with a big rock inconveniently in the middle of the channel, where the current boils one way when the tide floods and the other way when the tide ebbs. But we made it all right.

This was, indeed, a great adventure for me because I had never, except for the cruise to Australia, been anywhere else afloat except to San Pedro, Los Angeles, and the Hawaiian area. It was more like the milk run to me.

Q: What was the state of the naval base at Pearl in those prewar days?

Adm. W.: It was a very quiet, comfortable place to have duty. It was constantly being dredged and improved. We always understood that the defense of any base was up to the Army and not to the Navy, and this is still supposed to be the case, I believe. I'm not sure where the Air Force comes in in these days. In emergency, of course, as we all know, cooperation between the Army and the Navy in Hawaii was less than perfect, and cooperation between Washington and either or both of them was almost nonexistent.

Q: Did the fleet high command show any concern about the Japanese mandated islands? Was there any interest in learning what took place there?

Adm. W.: I never got to the Naval War College, but this was a matter of deep concern there, and I think all through the 1930s the No. 1 obsession at our Naval War College was a possible war with Japan. But this was in the ivory towers, and how far this actually got to the fleet — from my own experience I know it wasn't very far. Not as far as Withington was concerned!

Q: In your experience with the fleet there, what precautions were taken against a surprise attack?

Adm. W.: I should say none, none at all. There was concern about having a lot of ships bottled up in Pearl Harbor. In fact, we anchored in Lahaina Roads, off the island of Maui. This was one of the reasons we anchored there, and it was a sensible reason. Unfortunately, we were then wide open to torpedo attack by submarines! So — as you well know, no one ever gets something for nothing.

Q: Did we have organized reconnaissance flights?

Adm. W.: Yes. There was never enough available in the way of air planes. Indeed, I suppose there never will be to cover adequately large expanses of sea. But we tried, and all the exercises in the later years before World War II involved aerial scouting, both by our own seaplanes from the cruisers and battleships and from seaplanes. In those days there were mostly flying boats, although th were some seaplanes, I believe, that operated from land bases, not very many.

In the war games in and around the Hawaiian Islands, we used occasionally to include the Army, or be included by them, but never to any significant degree. There was one landing exercise on the west coast of Oahu, the worst possible beach for getting out of because it came right into, I think, it's called the Waianae Pocket. We actually carried some mules and landed them from 50-foot motor launches, and one or two of the hapless officers got kicked overboard by the mules. We didn't have any adequate boats, we didn't have adequate amphibious equipment of any sort, but we were at least aware that it might be necessary to land some troops somewhere some day, and we worked at it. All of the early development work for amphibious boats and ship types, as far as I know, was done at the schools at Quantico. I, as a naval ordnance officer, had nothing to do with that and had very little knowledge of it at the time. I was vaguely aware that it was going on, and I knew that there was nothing in the fleet of any capability at all, amphibiouswise.

Q: Was there any knowledge in the Pacific Fleet of the inadequacy of our torpedoes at that point?

Adm. W.: No. Unfortunately, there were never any live warhead shots fired. There were two reasons. Number one reason was that we couldn't get money out of Congress, and the second one was that the exploder was so highly classified that it was never ever allowed at sea, and this was the most fatuous error I ever heard of in my whole experience in the Navy. This is the reason we were caught with our pants off.

Q: Secrecy defeats itself!

Adm. W.: That's right. I believe to some extent this was also true later of the Norden bomb sight, which was a really fine small mechanism, but so highly classified that the pilots weren't adequately trained in its use when the war actually came. And in the early days of radar, the equipment which was designed basically in the Naval Research Laboratory, it was called the CXAM, was so highly classified that only the captain had the key to the radar shack on the ship! Astounding, but that's the way it went.

Q: Is there a more sensible attitude prevailing now?

Adm. W.: Yes and no. Officially there are some bad errors known to me. In electronic warfare, the two most concerned outfits are the ship people and the air people, and they're so highly classified that they very seldom talk to one another. This is still true, I understand. I believe that the present CNO has set up an electronics czar who's supposed to break this deadlock. I wish him well. Nobody else has been able to for a long period of years. The reason I speak from some knowledge, I've been concerned as a consultant in several different endeavors for the Navy since I retired - I guess five or six or seven - and one of the studies concerned missiles, and missiles inevitably concern countermeasures, electronic countermeasures, and we looked into this subject in some depth and we talked to both sides, but we couldn't get them to talk to each other. It's awfully discouraging how stupid people can be.

Well, where are we now?

Withington #1 - 43

Q: You want to tell me about your tour of duty in the Winslow.

Adm. W.: Yes, after I left Admiral Taussig. This was a very pleasant year based out of San Diego. We cruised through the Canal that year as far as the Virgin Islands, we got to Port Arthur, Texas, and we were supposed to go to New York - the whole fleet was supposed to go to New York and meet up with our brothers in the Atlantic Fleet. There was a war scare with Japan in early 1939, so we were all ordered back, boom, to the West Coast. No fooling! Meanwhile, all our families had gone east without any transportation money. I think my good father-in-law helped out, otherwise I would never have gotten my family back! No, I'm wrong about this. They came east, pulled up stakes, because they knew I was going ashore in June of 1939, and they stayed east while I went back west, and then I joined them and came back to duty in the Brueau of Ordnance in 1939.

Q: When you returned to the West Coast, Admiral Richardson was in command, was he?

Adm. W.: I think he was.

Q: What then took place in the face of this war scare?

Adm. W.: We in the Winslow went right back to San Diego, and I think almost all the destroyers. The Winslow was one of the so-called destroyer leaders of that type, with 5-inch guns that couldn't shoot against an airplane. They were surface guns only. One of the greatest mistakes the Navy Department ever made, because of the Bureau of Ordnance didn't have available a twin mount design.

Q: So they turned out new destroyers without anti-aircraft?

Adm. W.: All we had was the so-called 1.1, a quadruple mount which was a total failure. Admiral Blandy as World War II was imminent had to go to Europe and buy the Oerlikon 20-mm. and the Bofors 40-

Q: That was Swedish?

Adm. W.: Yes. In order to get close-range weapons for the fleet. Then we manufactured them in this country under license. But this was a gross failure on the part of the Bureau of Ordnance.

We did better, on the whole, in our fire control as World War loomed in front of us than we did in our guns or in our torpedoes. It was still before the days of the radar, and we still had the mechanical computer rather than the electronic computer. They were pretty reliable, well understood, and well made. The anti-aircraft computer, Mark I, was developed by Ford Instrument Company, now part of Sperry's, and eventually in World War II IBM made them as a sub-contractor with great difficulty, but they did. These computers were the basis of the 5-inch anti-aircraft and surface gun system in World War II. Within the limitations of the system, they were good. Everything worked.

This was my job when I went back to Washington in 1939, the fire control desk in the Bureau.

Q: Before that when you were still in the <u>Winslow</u> was there not some effort on the part of the ranking naval officers to exert pressure on Washington to do more in terms of guns?

Adm. W.: Yes, but this nemesis was still in the Bureau of Ordnance

They were beginning to reorganize, but it wasn't really reorganized until Admiral Blandy relieved as chief after the war broke. Then he did establish a research and development division on its own and each of the fire control outfits that were producing were paralleled in the research division by a development officer. And, I think it was pre World War II, Albert Einstein was once a consultant to the Bureau of Ordnance...

Q: He was at Princeton, then, was he?

Adm. W.: Yes, so was Dr. von Neumann, the great mathematician. I think this was just at the time when the importance of research and development was being realized in the Bureau of Ordnance and, to be fair, in the Navy as a whole. The bureau wasn't alone in this remissness, by any means.

Q: There's a great watershed there, just before we got in...

Adm. W.: Yes. In the late 1930s the Office of Naval Research began. For years the Naval Research Laboratory was an activity of the Bureau of Ships, then the Bureau of Engineering, Construction, and Repair. I forget which one of the bureaus before they merged was responsible for NRL. It was a very small activity, although they developed radar there independently, more or less, of the British, one of their notable accomplishments.

Q: This was a time when great things were happening at MIT.

Adm. W.: The Draper Laboratory called the Radiation Laboratory in the time of World War II - Draper did not have his laboratory.

then, I think. He was still a professor at MIT. He was the instructor-professor for all of the postgraduate officers at that time from the Navy.

Q: That's when they were learning about servo mechanisms?

Adm. W.: Yes. In the early days with radar, which occurred, of course, as World War II went on, this was one of my major concerns, managing somehow to get some black boxes into existing gun directors. And we did. A very able young man named Rivero, who's now Admiral Rivero in NATO, my No. 2 in the fire-control division, was very small, fortunately, and was able to crawl round inside of these directors with these wooden boxes in his hands trying to find a place to put them, and he did. And the radar, fairly good radar, I think it was called the Mark 35, was shoe-horned somehow onto the existing gun directors. It was quite a feat.

This is no slur on the Bureau of Ordnance because nobody knew anything about radar in time to develop it for World War II, most of all the Japanese, thank God, they were much later than we in developing it and it was quite crude even at the war end for them. This was one of the great advantages we had. This period in the Bureau of Ordnance as the war broke was a very hot one for everybody. There was almost nobody available there to work. It was expanding by leaps and bounds, and Reserve officers, among them Louis Strauss, who's a dear friend of mine today, came in from civilian life and the regulars sneaked off one by one as fast as they could to go to the war, leaving a bunch of Reserves! Which was, of course, the only way possible to run the Navy.

I was the duty officer in the Bureau of Ordnance the night

Pearl Harbor occurred. We were sweating blood in the Bureau of Ordnance as World War II broke. Naturally, I put on my uniform and went down to the Navy Department, where I was for the next 48 hours approximately.

I remember vividly that night receiving a request for 50-caliber machine gun ammunition. I started to act on these requests, then it occurred to me I'd better consult some higher authority. So I consulted then-Captain Holloway in Fleet Training and Fleet Operations, and I learned to my horror and informed him to his horror that the entire supply for the U.S. Navy was 500,000 rounds. This wasn't enough for more than a few days fighting. So he took over ladling out with a teaspoon the available resources, and I was relieved of this responsibility. I remember sometime about possibly four of five o'clock Monday morning, I looked up bleary-eyed from the chief's office where I was the duty officer and there was Louis Strauss with the first bitter story of the battleships sunk at Pearl Harbor. Neither of us could believe it, but of course it had happened.

I think that the war effort was generally a magnificent achievement in the Navy Department and, indeed, in the War Department also. Organizationally, there was only one god and his name was Ernie King and this was a good thing for the war and for the United States. The organization of what came to be called the Joint Chiefs, then the Combined Chiefs with the British, was sound. There were homeric differences of opinion, as I'm sure you know, especially between Admiral King and General Marshall, but the best officers in the Army and the Navy were available to assist the Chiefs, and the plans they generated and which were later approved by Mr. Roosevelt or, in the case of the Combined Chiefs by Mr. Churchill. As we know from 100 percent hindsight, it generally worked well and there's no more acid test for any war plan than that it actually worked in practice.

We were concerned in Ordnance which I was, of course, in part responsible for, about getting production started. All we could do was make more of what we knew how to make, obviously, so one day Commander France, who was my boss in fire control, called in the responsible representatives of the Ford Instrument Company, the Control Instrument Company, the General Electric Company, and one or two other big companies, turned off all tape recorders, and started out by saying "if anybody quoted me about anything that happened in this meeting I would deny it and call him a liar." Then I doled out all the business I knew was going to be necessary - so many range finders, so many range keepers, so many computers, so many gun sights, and so on and so on down the line.

Q: When did this take place? How much after Pearl Harbor?

Adm. W.: It couldn't have been more than a month after Pearl Harbor.

Q: How did you manage to make all these estimates in that period of time?

Adm. W.: The Navy expansion was then well under way, fortunately for the country, and unlimited amounts of money had been made available. It was just a matter of implementing what had to be done. Everybody produced according to the schedule they agreed to and we had the equipment ready for the ships when they were commissioned. The crews weren't nearly as well ready as the equipment was, as it turned out.

Q: The manpower factor was much more difficult than the production?

Adm. W.: Much more difficult. As we found out later, this was very painful because a battleship crew got depleted every quarter, and certainly every six months, as we'd send nucleus crews to start another ship. This was the only possible method, but it kept the fighting efficiency of all the older ships at a relatively low level, so that everybody fought at more or less the same low level of experience.

Q: When did the build-up in Ordnance begin?

Adm. W.: Let me see, I came to the Bureau in 1939. It began more or less simultaneously with my arrival. I forget the sequence. There was a Vinson-Trammell Act and there was NRA. Roosevelt illegally made a lot of money available to the Army and Navy through the relief appropriations. Indeed, the quarters on Ford Island were made out of plans for Alaska, with roofs that could take four feet of snow, because they couldn't afford to pay an architect, but they had some money to build the quarters with from relief funds and made work for people.

Q: This was understood by the Congress, in part at least, wasn't it?

Adm. W.: I think so. For instance, Congressman Shepherd, for many years in the Congress, was on the Naval Appropriations Committee and always knew everything about the Navy and where the money came from, especially. He was on the Appropriations Sub-committee. No, nobody was fooled, and they were glad to have it done, I think.

Q: Carl Vinson was very close to FDR, was he not?

Adm. W.: Yes, but the boys who controlled the money were even closer to the actual events than Carl who was on the Naval Affairs Committee. He was a policy guy, but he didn't appropriate the money. The military had been aware, of course, since World War II broke out that we might be involved at any time, and so was the President, and more and more so with the Congress. If you remember, they barely passed the draft call by one or two votes, mighty close.

Q: And there was a great battle over the fifty destroyers, I remember.

Adm. W.: Yes -

Q: This sub rosa way of operating and making funds available was due in part to the fact that public opinion hadn't progressed?

Adm. W.: Oh, yes. Roosevelt, if you remember, made a "quarantine the aggressors" speech in Chicago which laid a large egg, and he had to draw in his horns because he felt, and accurately felt, that he had no public support. Mr. Stimson looked at Manchuria and knew everything that the Japanese were doing right along, but he couldn't generate any heat for us to do anything about it. Of course, the League of Nations did nothing either.

A little more about this conference to divide up the business for fire control: what my object was was to work them all to their absolute limit of capacity. This was the only way we could get the equipment, and it worked. Fortunately, nobody defaulted.

Q: What sort of deadlines did you assign?

Adm. W.: They didn't have to be too unreasonable. It takes a long time to build a ship, even under wartime conditions, so this was not too difficult.

Q: And the orders you were giving out to the various industries required expansion on their part, did it not?

Adm. W.: Yes. They all screamed that they couldn't do it, but they all managed to do it. There was a certain amount of capacity still left in the Navy yards for back up, but not very much. By and large, this had to be an industry operation.

Q: In terms of time, what were you thinking about? A year? A year and a half, or what?

Adm. W.: Yes. No, that's not quite so. We had a projected building program which went as much as three years in the future because some of the big battleships were in it, you see, and aircraft carriers are not evolved overnight. But we didn't foresee the enormous number of amphibious ships that were going to be built, and these orders had constantly to be expanded and modified to take care of the increasing requirements. Naturally, an LCI, for instance, or an LCU, requires very little in the way of fire control, but they all require machine guns. I was not concerned with these in the Bureau, but somebody was.

Q: At that early period when we were just getting involved in the war ourselves, there must have been heavy demands on us by the British for equipment.

Adm. W.: Yes.

Q: How did you deal with that? How did you allocate that?

Adm. W.: This was, of course, beyond my level and as it happened the fire-control business was not concerned, but there were massive amounts of ammunition required, and I believe that in case of real dispute as to claimants as between ourselves and the British or the French, the problem sometimes had to go all the way up through the Joint Chiefs to the Combined Chiefs and occasionally to the White House and Churchill. The business of diverting equipment to Russia via the North Cape convoys was a very difficult one, not only because of the heavy losses, but because of the diversion of equipment. These were high policy matters. We just sweated to get everything we could as fast as we could and hope that it would work.

Q: Yes, because when it came down to you, you had to make the consignments and the requests in terms of volume and so forth.

Adm. W.: That's right. Also, everything was informal and speeded up. I used to hand-carry the contracts down to my opposite number in the Bureau of Supplies and Accounts and stand there while he signed them. Things were that urgent. Fortunately, there were no serious slips. I never heard of any in this process, but of course it wasn't a proper safeguard for public property anyway, but it got things done that had to be done.

Withington #1 - 53

Q: How did you circumvent the legal requirements for competitive bids and that kind of thing?

Adm. W.: We just ignored them. I told you about this quite illegal conference I had with industry.

Q: And that's what you were doing...

Adm. W.: That's what I did, yes. Otherwise, we wouldn't have had any equipment. This was generally accepted as a necessity. There was some waste, of course, but I never heard of any major scandal. I don't know of any major scandal. A good many incompetent contractors failed to produce, but this was not a scandal. You just had to bet on any reasonable looking horse that could walk, and maybe he could run and maybe he couldn't.

Q: Well, in those early days it was a question of national survival, wasn't it?

Adm. W.: Certainly, of course. They were mighty black days in 1942 and 1943. I was anxious to get out and into the war like everybody else, and I did reasonably well. I finally was ordered to a battleship in March 1942 which was, of course, a very sensible thing to do in view of my whole professional background. I was ordered to the USS Indiana at Newport News as gunnery officer.

Q: Let me interject a question at this point. You were anxious to get out and you had developed certain skills in ordnance and awarding contracts and so forth. Is it not a waste to permit men to go out and take up some other assignment?

Adm. W.: This is really a bigger question. Should the material specialist be a line officer at all? This is really your question. My own feeling is "yes." I'm afraid that the present tendency is in the opposite direction. You undoubtedly read that the present regime in the Navy Department has told the Selection Board - you don't have to consider command necessary at sea before you select a man for promotion to flag rank. The proper answer, of course, is somewhere in between the two extremes. Nobody can be promoted unless he's commanded ships, or everybody can be promoted whatever he has failed to command. I've always felt that in ordnance especially the only way to develop a responsible, effective corps of officers was to order them occasionally to sea to use their product, and, by God, if it didn't work it was their baby and they had to make it work. There's a great deal of force in this though I think.

Q: You were then an original Opdevfor man?

Adm. W.: Yes. I never have been Opdevfor, but I highly approved of the organization and the outfit.

Q: Isn't it true that as a result of the expansion of the Navy in World War II we inevitably began to turn toward specialization?

Adm. W.: We had to. It was impossible to train the Reserve officers for more than one thing, and the Reserve officers who came into the bureaus of the Navy Department never went to sea at all. There wasn't any point in sending them, but increasingly they got enough expertise and ability so that line officers who were doing the job originally could be released to go to sea, and this was the deal in my case and the case of many others. It was on the whole, I think, a sensible procedure.

Q: Were you able to turn over your particular job in production to somebody equally well qualified?

Adm. W.: It was Frank Hanafee, who was class of 1917, and who had been out of the Navy for many years. He came back as a Reserve officer and was thoroughly qualified. So the answer to your questions is yes, I did have a qualified relief, a man who was never considered as a possibility for going to sea in the war.

Q: Because in leaving a situation like that at a crucial time you weren't able to pass on your contacts you'd made and that sort of thing?

Adm. W.: He'd been in the office with me for more than a year as a junior, you see, so that the transition for him was not difficult at all. In many cases it was most difficult for other officers, but not as it happened here. By that time also the development of optics and fire control was in the research division, and I was only the producer, so that the original responsibility at the start of the war for everything had been dissipated, and sensibly so.

Q: I believe that Admiral King must have thought in these lines, because his policy was to try to hang on to his men on his staff and not let them go.

Adm. W.: Yes, that's true. He also was his own one-man selection board. I never understood, and I don't think anybody else ever did either, How the flag officers evolved, and every once in a while if somebody made a grievous error or grounded a ship, he got quietly taken off Admiral King's list and was not made a flag officer. I don't believe there was ever any formal selection process during World War II for flag rank. Ernie was it.

I never worked so hard in my life as I did during those first months of the war in the Bureau of Ordnance. The specifications were not ready for these contracts, so I wrote them at night at home, and we had grossly inadequate assistance. The Reserve officers were just beginning to come in and buy their caps and uniforms but they weren"t there yet, and the work involved was very heavy for a period of about a year. As I remember, we didn't have any breakdowns among the handful of knowledgeable, competent officers in the Bureau, but I don't know why we didn't. The strain was fearful.

Q: Well, weren't we all sort of carried along by this joint...

Adm. W.: You expected to work all day every day and all night every night.

Q: Exactly. It demanded it and...

Adm. W.: Yes. I don't know why I didn't get my ulcer then, but I didn't until after I became chief of the Bureau. That was quite a long time later.

The first skipper of the Indiana was Captain Merrill who later became Admiral Merrill, a famous wartime South Pacific commander. One of the most charming and able men I've ever had the good fortune to be with. He loved us all and we loved him. He let us alone to do our work. It's pretty hard to say anything better about any man.

The fitting-out period in Newport News and in the Bay area was not easy. I remember the first time we started to train the turrets — that is, to move them — the relative hardness between the rollers and the roller pads was wrong, and the word came over the loudspeaker, "Fire in turret one." There was so much friction that smoke billowed out. It was necessary to raise the turret and re-machine the roller paths and change the hardness of the rollers before the turret could be trained properly. This was damned discouraging to the captain and the gunnery officer, I assure you. That was our major problem, I think, and it was a big one. It delayed us, of course, getting ready to go out to the South Pacific.

Because the submarine menace off the Capes was so imminent, and real, we had to do our shooting, including 16-inch guns, inside Chesapeake Bay.

Q: That was your shakedown?

Adm. W.: That was our shakedown.

Q: That was difficult to achieve, wasn't it?

Adm. W.: Yes. We didn't kill anybody, fortunately. We didn't commit any serious wild shots. I remember going into each turret with each green turret crew and officer, as the gunnery officer, the first time they fired, but nobody had panicked, and nobody did.

Q: What new equipment was the _Indiana_ carrying?

Adm. W.: There wasn't anything new, really. It was a development of the later 1930s with main battery directors, the 5-inch directors.

Withington #1 - 58

We had by that time the 40-mm. and 20-mm. guns that Admiral Blandy had bought the rights to in Sweden and Switzerland. We had a good outfit, less radar. There wasn't any radar.

Q: The Washington was equipped with radar, was she not?

Adm. W.: I think so. How and in what sequence we got the radar is not too clear to me. Wait a minute. We started out with a crude form of an SG radar, that is a surface search. We had a crude form of an air search.

Q: A great super...

Adm. W.: That's right, bed spring. It was only as the war progressed that the Bureau was able to produce radars for the gun directors. The shift had to be the air-search radar at the foremast of the Indiana. This was done in Noumea, New Caledonia, by a brilliant young naval constructor with a sky hook. I don't know to this day how he did it because he had no Navy yard facilities of any sort whatever—

Q: Who was he?

Adm. W.: Cowdrey, class of 1920. Somehow he managed to do this. The captain wouldn't even come out and look. I did. The captain couldn't bear it!

During my time in the ship, we did not have any gun director radars. We did have air and surface search of an early and fairly crude type.

Q: What kind of damage control?

Adm. W.: We had an excellent damage control organization and excellent damage-control equipment in the ship. There was a damage-control center and proper communications.

We didn't go to the South Pacific until the end of 1942 and by this time we'd lost some carriers by fire and we knew the hard way what had to be done and were doing it.

Q: Did you carry spare parts and that kind of thing?

Adm. W.: There was surprisingly a happy situation in the guesses the Bureaus of Ships and Ordnance had to make as to what spare parts we needed. We were very well equipped. We almost never were down for lack of parts. Of course, one big reason for this was that we didn't have much electronic equipment back then, except radios, and they were pretty well known.

Q: But isn't it true also that some of the equipment that you carry, extra equipment, is due largely to the foresight of the officers on the ships?

Adm. W.: To some extent in those days, to no extent now. They have a so-called provisioning conference during the development of new weapons, weapons systems, and everybody with any knowledge or experience sits around a table and makes out the spare parts list for the ship, the tender, and the Navy yard.

Q: That's what exists now?

Adm. W.: Yes. This has existed for many years and it essentially did exist in those days. You had to have a list because this was the basis for the budget request, and still is. Then, if the budget request is cut, you're short of parts. Aeronautics has been plagued by this for years, much more so than ordnance or ships, I think. Inadequate spare parts. Knowingly inadequate from the start, and Congress won't listen in some cases.

Q: Were there any bugs that you discovered in Chesapeake Bay during the shake-down?

Adm. W.: No. There were a great many deficiencies in training which, of course, we had to work on all the time.

Q: What kind of complement did you have?

Adm. W.: All the men we needed, but they didn't know anything, most of them. I guess maybe 2,400 officers and men, or something of that sort. We had a very fine competent, experienced nucleus of men and a few experienced officers. I think we had one Naval Academy graduate of the class of 1942. Contrast this with the <u>West Virginia</u> with 30 from the class of 1923. This was the problem, you see.

Q: There weren't enough to go around.

Adm. W.: We had all these willing young Reserves and that was it. They had to run the ship. In fact, they won the war, by and large, as you well know. The professionals fortunately didn't make too many mistakes.

Q: The Reservists brought a wealth of experience, didn't they?

Adm. W.: In some cases, yes, in most cases, no. Especially the officers on the LSTs and the amphibious types. They didn't know anything. How they ever got from Panama to Hawaii and the South

Pacific I'll never know.

Q: I was thinking of on the battleships where you had a large group of Reservists, then the composite knowledge and experience they brought must have been useful.

Adm. W.: Yes. We went out to the South Pacific by way of Fiji in company with the cruiser Columbia. One of the officers on the Columbia was Robert Montgomery who was then a Captain, U.S. Naval Reserve. We stopped in Fiji and went ashore and met some of the nurses. There was great excitement, seeing females, but the No. 2 doctor traded his curettes for all of the blood they had - this was an Army hospital and it had no patients. They were way back in the rear, you see, and they did have some pregnant nurses! When these girls saw Robert Montgomery they just wouldn't believe it. Quite an experience.

We passed on the way out, in the same anchorage, the South Dakota which had just had the hell shot out of her during one of these bitter battles in the Solomons. She was going home for repairs. The captain had been wounded and the executive officer was in command of the ship, which had been hit forty times, I think, in a night action. But she'd done a lot of hitting, too, and she'd come out all right. She went on throughout the whole war and had a very distinguished record.

Q: When you were ready to go out to the Pacific, what sort of an escort did you have?

Adm. W.: I think we had maybe one destroyer with us. I forget now. Maybe two. They were also joining up. We were in the new-fashioned term a task group. There wasn't any air cover except the planes that the cruiser and the battleship carried.

Q: But, as you said, the submarine menace at that time in the Atlantic was real.

Adm. W.: It was real. In the Pacific in the area where we were, it was non-existent essentially, and we knew that.

Q: What special precautions, what kind of an escort did you have in the Atlantic on the way down to the Canal?

Adm. W.: I think one or two destroyers, that's all.

Q: You relied on speed, then?

Adm. W.: Oh, sure. And speed is, as you know, the best defense against especially the World War II submarine with low sustained underwater speed - six, seven, or eight knots for a limited period.
We spent much of our time right in the harbor of Noumea, New Caledonia. We did get up toward The Slot repeatedly, but we were never in any of the actions in the _Indiana_. There were actions while we were there and bitter battles and grievous losses, but we never happened to be in them.

Q: How do you account for that?

Adm. W.: Pure chance.

Q: You weren't being held in reserve or anything?

Adm. W.: Oh, no. We were out there in the area in support three, four, or five times, But it never turned out to be a fleet action at any time during this period. We got up as far as Efate in the New Hebrides once or twice, and this became a forward base instead of Noumea as the war progressed. We were the heavy support, but were never called upon during my time in the ship.

We went up to Pearl Harbor once for an interim overhaul, and on the way there or back we bombarded Nauru, which is a tiny dot of land in the South Pacific, where the Japanese had phosphate mines.

Q: But not many defenses, did they?

Adm. W.: We didn't have any bombardment projectiles, so we fired AP. It was great for our morale, but I'm sure we did no harm. I'm not even sure the fuses would go off, by design, you see, hitting into the dirt instead of armor plate. They did shoot back at us, and one destroyer, whose captain was U. S. Grant Sharp, later the commander-in-chief in the Pacific, got hit with loss of men, and had to creep out of range.

Q: We speak of not knowing whether the 16-inch shells exploded, they didn't under other circumstances, too, I believe. The Massachusetts had this experience in North Africa.

Adm. W.: But again this was not entirely the fault of the designers, because they weren't designed to explode on contact with dirt. They were supposed to penetrate armor plate and then explode.

Q: In the case of the Massachusetts they did penetrate the Jean Bart's armor but -

Adm. W.: Didn't explode!

Withington #1 - 64

Q: I know because I got the repercussions to that.

Adm. W.: It's just astonishing how many failures we had, very discouraging. The ordnance people, officers on duty in Ordnance, were always hopefully carefully selected, among the top men in their classes. They were supposed to come across with the very best of all kinds of equipment.

Towards the end of my service in the Indiana, we were in the Gilberts operations and then, by that time, the task group organization was in effect. We were in a screen with destroyers, other battleships and cruisers, around the carriers. Admiral Sherman was our task group commander. We were not concerned with the bombardment of Tarawa - that's one of the islands ....

Q: And that's where the pillboxes were.

Adm. W.: Yes. Let me see. Where was it where Colonel Shoup was ashore, and Admiral Hill was in command in the Maryland bombarding them? The island where the losses to the Second Marine Division were so grievous.

Q: It was Makin, wasn't it?

Adm. W.: No, it was Tarawa. Makin was attacked first by Carlson's Raiders and the Fifth Army Group. The bombardment of this little tiny island was thought to be quite sufficient, but most of the shells ricocheted off. This was in the Gilberts. I was only there as I say, in the Indiana in this task group as distant support and saw nothing of the action at all.

Q: How far off did you stand?

Adm. W.: We never saw any land at all. They used the old battleships like the Maryland as part of the bombardment forces throughout the Pacific war. It was very seldom that the fast battleships got to bombard. Only toward the end did they bombard some steel plants in Japan.

Q: Why was this?

Adm. W.: They were needed to screen the carriers and to meet the Japanese fleet.

We are now at a turning point in my life in World War II. My detachment orders from the Indiana. I had never met Admiral Harry Hill at all. I knew him only slightly by reputation, when I received a message aboard the Indiana, then being executive officer, to report to him as chief of staff. I had not even yet been promoted to captain. I was pretty sure I was going to be, but nothing official had happened. We were then in the South Pacific at Efate and I was relieved by, oddly enough, the then gunnery officer who fleeted up to executive officer, just as I had done in my turn. My captain, Captain William F. Fechteler, was relieved, unfortunately for the ship, I think, the same day that I was. We left the ship together. This is no way to run a ship in the middle of a war, or any other time - to detach Nos. 1 and 2 simultaneously. The fact that the ship was in a grievous collision shortly thereafter was quite beside the point, but it does seem somehow to underline the basic fact that the top man if he has to be relieved, and of course he has to be relieved periodically, should never be relieved simultaneously with No. 2.

Q: How did this happen?

Withington #1 - 66

Adm. W.: It was pure chance, I think. Orders sometimes came from Washington in those days, sometimes from the commander-in-chief, Nimitz and his staff in Pearl Harbor, and somebody made a stupid, stupid error. Anyway, I flew by PBY from Efate in the New Hebrides to Pearl Harbor, it's my recollection at this late date, at 75 knots and with numerous stops it took three days.

Q: I hope your navigator was good!

Adm. W.: We did not get lost. A Navy nurse who was traveling even further, from Australia, got very air sick, I remember, during the passage, but otherwise it was not of any moment except the eternal monotony of it. I reported to Harry Hill for duty as his chief of staff in Honolulu. He and the amphibious force was in a transport called the Cambria, and this was a completely new world to this battleships, ordnance sailor, Withington. I knew nothing, really, about the amphibious Navy at all, except what I had read and studied.

Q: How did you happen to be selected, then, to be his chief of staff?

Adm. W.: His previous chief of staff at Tarawa had been worn out previously by duty in the destroyer battles in the Solomons. He was literally worn out, mentally and physically, and had to be relieved, and he recommended me to Admiral Hill. Tommy Ryan, class of 1921. Why my name should have occurred to him, I don't know. ~~We had never been particularly close or particular friends.~~ These coincidences happen in the Navy, as they happen all through our lives, of course. I never regretted the fact that Tom did so recommend me. I've always been grateful to him for the recommendation.

Harry Hill was a bouncing, able, brilliant man, full of life and go and zing, eager to learn all he could about this new art of amphibious warfare. Handsome Harry! He never walked up a gangway, he always ran up a gangway no matter how high it was. No height was ever too steep for Harry to scale. He never admitted that height even existed. A wonderful man to work for, a very exacting and sometimes a very trying taskmaster, but I learned greatly from him as I had before from Admiral Taussig.

Our first wartime activity was more or less of a crashing anticlimax. We were to attack the atoll of Majuro allegedly filled with Japs. We arrived there to bombard the island which, of course, was densely clothed in coconut palms and underbrush. We entered a lagoon which had been mapped from aerial photographs only, so that the coral showed in the colored photographs - the United States having no charts of this lagoon - we entered the lagoon, landed the landing force, and found no Japanese there watsoever!

Q: You'd driven them into the earth!

Adm. W.: They weren't there. Our intelligence was grievously at fault. This was a supporting and minor operation previous to the attack on Kwajalein, which we had no part in at all. Having secured the atoll, we proceeded to Kwajalein arriving there before the battle was over. We had with us the Kwajalein reserve of troops in several transports. These men were not needed for the Kwajalein assault landings. Quite on the spur of the moment Admiral Spruance and his staff and the Marines and their people decided we should go on a thousand miles farther toward Japan and capture the atoll of Eniwetok. While Kwajalein was being secured, we were planning under forced draft to take the reserve to attack Eniwetok.

This was done with a combined force of Marines and Army under the command of a Marine Corps general. For the first time in this island-hopping war in the Pacific, it was decided, and Admiral Hill as the attack force commander made the decision, to enter the atoll first and then to fight, rather than fighting from outside the atoll and entering later. This proved to be a brillia success. We passed through the eastern entrance of the atoll of Eniwetok, knowing damn well that the Japanese at the end of their guns were looking down our throats in the jungle. They never fire a shot at us. Why, I shall never know. The operation, as I recal lasted three days, starting with the attack on the end of the isla at the northern end of the lagoon ...

Q: What's the island?

Adm. W.: Engebi. I forget whether this was the code name or the real name. It doesn't matter any more. This was the island on which there then existed a small, short runway, and after this island was captured with almost no prisoners because all the Japanese fought to the death, we moved inside the lagoon south to the main island to Eniwetok, where the main action occurred. Here the green Army troops did not do very well, and had to be reinforc by the tired Marines who had already battled for the northern isla

At the end of three days, all three islands, the third one being Parry Island, just to the north of Eniwetok, were secured and we soon started back to Honolulu to plan for the next operation.

Q: Tell me, what kind of shore guns did the Japs have?

Adm. W.: Very small-caliber guns. In fact, I don't remember any splashes around us at all, they were so poorly armed. I suspect that whatever they had in the way of artillery was sighted to seaward, more or less the way the British were caught at Singapore, and they couldn't shoot toward the lagoon.

Q: Was our action, then, in going into the lagoon predicated on the intelligence we had?

Adm. W.: We had very good intelligence as to the numbers and their equipment and their armament. They fought tenaciously, as they did everywhere in the Pacific. Lots of Japanese on the main island of Eniwetok, which incidentally is the highest island in the Marshalls - it's nine feet above sea level at the high point - were hidden in so-called spider holes. In other words, cylindrical holes tall enough for a man with a little cap of vegetation over it, a man-made device, a trap. The occupant, the Japanese soldier, would wait until the attack troops had gone over and then flip up the lid of vegetation and stealthily stab us in the back. This was not very good for the morale of the American attackers, but there was only a handful of these men, and they were soon tracked down and killed.

Q: How had we obtained our intelligence on the Japanese?

Adm. W.: As you know, we had broken the Japanese code and to some extent we learned from that. More importantly, we captured in Kwajalein atoll a small Japanese ship which had the latest char[ts] of all the islands in the Japanese-held territory.

Q: You mean, gun emplacements and that sort of thing?

Adm. W.: No, but the navigation details were all there. Gun emplacements were largely a matter of guesswork, plus the dispatch intelligence from the attacking planes and bombarding ships which observed these islands previous to the landing attempts. This actual intelligence from gun flashes was the best we had, and, of course, it was up to date within a few days of the date of the actual landing.

Once or twice some intelligence got lost, and our ships were hit because they weren't ever informed that these flashes had been observed and where they'd been observed. This happened later at Tinian. The actual intelligence of where the defenders were from their own gun flashes was obtained partially by aviators attacking and secondarily by the bombarding ships. As you probably know, th[e] old battleships became exceedingly adept at bombardment and they used the gunsights. They came at point-blank range to shoot at these low driblets of land in the vast expanse of the sea. Otherwise, it was impossible to make a hit. And by that time the battl[e] ships did have adequate bombardment ammunition, high-capacity, hig[h] explosive, and it did explode when it hit these bits of land in the ocean.

The whole Eniwetok operation was a fast operation and a great success and made Admiral Hill's reputation. He was shortly therea[fter] made a vice admiral. One of my fond recollections is of the fabulous beachmaster called Squeaky Anderson. You've probably heard of him. He became eventually a Rear Admiral, U. S. Naval Reserve. He ran away from Sweden after he'd been caught getting a girl pregnant, and sailed before the mast and deserted in San Francisco, and thereafter made his way somehow to Alaska, where he by his own bare-handed effort became a very successful man in the fishing industry. He knew the islands thoroughly, and he was first enlisted by the Navy to be the beachmaster in the attack on the god-forsaken island of Attu in the Aleutian Islands. He was so successful here that his reputation in the Navy was made. He was then made an officer by acclamation, and Harry Hill somehow smelled him out and he was his beachmaster at Makin atoll, and thereafter at Eniwetok, Saipan, and Tinian. After I left Admiral Hill he was beachmaster at Iwo Jima.

So, we had now successfully attacked Eniwetok and were going home to Pearl, and Admiral Hill is counting on Captain Withington to get the action reports out before we get back to Honolulu, which we did by a great effort. At this point, Admiral Hill was thoughtful enough to dream up a mission for Withington in Washington. I had been away from my wife and family for the better part of two years. He knew that I was a walking battle-fatigue case, so he decided that he would do something about it, and I went to Washington by air with a high-sounding set of orders, but nothing really to do seriously, except to get re-acquainted with my wife and children. And I've always been grateful to Harry Hill ever since for his thoughtfulness.

Q: It's interesting that he himself never did that.

Adm. W.: I know it. He never came home, as far as I know. There were a couple of things that he wanted to know that were of some moment regarding the future of the Pacific war that somebody else could have gotten just as well as I.

I came back greatly refreshed from the interlude in the United States and quite shocked by having been saluted by the WAVES on the streets of San Francisco, having never seen a WAVE before! Then the planning started for a much larger operation for the capture of Saipan. This involved three Marine divisions, thirty-six LSTs, and a huge armada of aircraft carriers, old battleships, fast battleships, LCIs, LCTs - the greatest armada that up to then had been assembled in the war for an amphibious operation. The preparatory drills were held largely in the Hawaiian Islands. Somehow or other Tokyo Rose, this traitor woman on the radio in Tokyo, had some suspicion through the Japanese intelligence that an operation was impending and she said on the radio "such and such men of the Marines Fourth Division are about to attack. The veterans one year hence will hold a rendezvous and a meeting in a telephone booth." This was very effective propaganda. I was sort of glad at the time I was not a Marine. They all laughed it off, or at least pretended to. They often responded in great numbers to the church call onSunday. This was one of the facts of the war which impressed me greatly. When a man's life is in danger, he thinks about God. Normally, he wouldn't consider his future or any possible higher authority in any way.

Q: Don't you think this is true in civilian life as well? Did you see any of the Japanese leaflets - propaganda leaflets - whic were dropped and very much in the same vein as what you were recounting about Tokyo Rose?

Adm. W.: I have in my papers somewhere the translation by the Marine Corps of the last message which General Saito on Saipan addressed to his men. They were a composite of Japanese service troops, Army and Marines and a few stray aviators, and maybe, a few civilians. Admitting that the end was near, this overpowering force which we had at Saipan had been too much, there was nothing left to do but to die for the emperor, and three cheers and a banzai for the emperor. This message was written and distributed and shortly after he himself with the assistance of his chief of staff committed hari-kari, as many of the Japanese military commanders did during the Pacific war. Japanese military tradition refused to admit defeat, refused to accept the fact that a man could surrender. This is the main reason that there were so few Japanese captured during World War II. They didn't necessarily disembowel themselves with a sharp knife in the traditional bushido way, but they would shoot themselves or shoot one another in order to avoid capture.

The preparations for Saipan were, of course, massive because so many ships and men were involved.

Q: They were all accomplished while you were at Pearl, were they?

Adm. W.: Yes, all the planning was done at Pearl.

Q: Who else sat in, Kelly Turner?

Adm. W.: Kelly Turner was the head man. I was deputized by him, although I was Harry Hill's chief of staff, to prepare a voluminous plan for running the island after it was captured, and I remember being called over by Admiral Turner, who was very overpowering indeed, and being generally complimented for my work. This was surprising since he almost never had a good word for anybody!

Q: What kind of an administrative plan did you set up?

Adm. W.: What the port director would do after Saipan was captured, how he would run the place, how the mail service would be handled, the details just go on and on - garbage, trash, you just name it - how you run a town. This is what the plan amounted to. And the Army general who was to be the island governor after the place was captured would use this book as his bible. Of course, as circumstances dictated, he would modify the instructions as necessary. But it was necessary to have a really basic document started so that everybody knew what was supposed to happen.

The preparations at Pearl Harbor were almost complete when there was a massive and catastropic explosion on board an LST, in the west loch, at Pearl Harbor. Some of the heavy artillery, 155, were in this ship, the ammunition was improperly and carelessly handled, and the ship just blew sky high, with severe damage to other ships. This impaired the amount of artillery available for the expedition, but the expedition went on anyhow, after everybody had picked up the corpses and the pieces from this massive explosion.

Q: By that time the supply of artillery was becoming more plentiful anyway, wasn't it?

Adm. W.: Oh, yes, but every piece was important. Later on, after Saipan was captured, there were 150 artillery pieces lined up on the south coast bombarding Tinian during the assault landing on Ti

So every one of those barrels that did not come as a result of this explosion was missed that day. The whole Saipan operation was a rather text-book affair from an amphibious warfare point of view. Losses ashore were heavy on both sides. The island itself is quite large and mountainous and a splendid target both for bombardment from the air and from the sea, and the bombardments in the event, on D-day, when the assault occurred, proved to be rather adequate in taking out most of the major targets, most of the major defense installations. Although there was considerable artillery fire against the initial assault landing waves, which took place in LVTs, the tracked vehicles, because they all had to cross a coral reef. The fight at Saipan took two weeks and it went on in dilatory fashion for many weeks later after the island had been declared officially secure, because of the intractable small clumps of Japanese military who hid out and refused to surrender and kept on shooting every chance they had.

q: They were in a series of caves.

Adm. W.: Yes, and the civilians and their families unhappily believed the Japanese propaganda that they'd be raped and killed and murdered and butchered by the Americans, particularly the black Americans. Many of them jumped off the cliffs into the sea and committeed suicide. This was one of the saddest stories of the whole Pacific war.

We had boats equipped with loud-hailers and broadcast the messages in the vernacular language telling these people, for God's sake come on in, we'll feed you, and take care of you. But they refused to believe it, and many, many civilians and essentially all the Japanese military who weren't killed in action jumped into the sea. The number of people actually captured in the military was miniscule and the number of civilians was comparatively small. This was, I guess, the bloodiest action in numbers as of that date in the Pacific war. In unit casualties, I think Tarawa may have been the bloodiest of all, but I'm not sure. Iwo Jima was very high, too.

Q: Tarawa was the surprise element.

Adm. W.: It wasn't really a surprise because there was a preliminary bombardment which hadn't been very effective because the targets were so minute. But the number of casualties per attacking unit I believe was the highest at Tarawa of anywhere else in the war.

Q: Admiral, what was your reaction, emotionally speaking, to an engagement like Saipan? The duration and the slaughter and what-have-you?

Adm. W.: I was not then and am not now really a critic of land warfare. The Army has always claimed - stated, I should say - that the Marine Corps in order to attain quick results will accept too high a casualty rate, and there was a great battle between the services on the island of Saipan. The Army 25th Division between the two Marine divisions, the 2nd and the 4th, lagged behind, the flanks were left in the air. In the end Admiral Spruance relieved the division commander, General Smith, and put the Army general who was there to command the island after it was captured - I think his name was Jarman - in command of the 25th Division. This created enormous bad feeling between the Army and the Navy on the sp and throughout the war in the Pacific thereafter. As I say, I'm no expert on land warfare. I don't know whether General Howling Mad Smith and Admiral Spruance were justified in this or not, but they did it.

Three divisions of men in U. S. terms meant upwards of 40,000 combat soldiers on this small island. This was a large and bloody and costly operation.

Q: Do you want to talk about the role of the Seabees?

Adm. W.: They were not of any great consequence either here or at Tinian, during the assault phase. The underwater demolition teams, yes. They worked on the reefs under fire with gun support from the sea, from our ships, looking for explosives, looking for underwater obstacles, and blowing channels where it was clear they should be blown. Utterly fearless men of all services! Most of them were Army. The best swimmers of any service and the bravest men. I don't know where they had their toughest role to play in the war. Possibly at Iwo Jima, but I was not present, having been sent back to Washington by that time. I always thought that they were the bravest men in the whole war.

After Saipan, the island immediately to the south, Tinian, was assaulted, using the reserve force which had not been needed at Saipan. Admiral Hill was placed entirely in command of the Tinian operation, whereas Admiral Turner had been actually in command at Saipan. This was a rather simple tactical operation since there was only a half-mile or so of water between one place and the other. It was decided to attack over a small beach near the northern end of the island rather than at the southern end, where there was a town and a good beach, and this worked, although the beach was exceedingly narrow, on the order, maybe, of 100 yards, and the better part of a division of men went through there on the assaulting day.

I think I mentioned earlier that the assault was supported by gunfire and, of course, aviation. During the actual assault, from the flank across the strait between Saipan and Tinian 150 guns, largely manned by the Army, and firing with complete certainty that they weren't going to hurt the assault force because they were on the flank, made this operation more or less a walk-off- There were very few casualties on D-day in the assaulting Marine force. The Japanese were quite surprised since they never expected an attack at that beach. They had put a few land mines out in the sand and in the water, and one or two of our amphibious vehicles were blown up early in the assault, but this is all that happened, really.

The Tinian operation was a great success with a minimum number of casualties, and, as you will remember, this later became with the enlargement of the airfields the bomber base from which Japan was bombarded and from which one of the planes with the atomic bomb took off for Japan. The Tinian operation and the Saipan operation were both more or less concurrent with the assault on Guam by a different outfit under Admiral Conolly, under the direct general command of Admiral Kelly Turner and of Admiral Spruance.

I should comment before leaving this subject on Admiral Spruance and the responsibility he felt for the Marines ashore on Saipan. It was known that the Japanese Navy was moving in our direction from the Philippines. Admiral Spruance withdrew the task forces with the heavy carriers and the battleships and cruisers and most of the destroyers to interpose between this attacking Japanese force and Saipan. He refused to be drawn far enough away from Saipan so that any unknown but resolute force of Japanese Navy ships from the home islands could come in behind him and get at us off the beach. I know quite well what I'm speaking of because I was with Harry Hill in the flagship Cambria exposed off the beach supporting the Marines while we were naked. Two or three Japanese destroyers could have beaten the hell out of us.

Admiral Spruance has been violently criticized for over-caution in not sinking the Japanese Navy ships coming from the Philippines, but he didn't know at the time that this was the entire effective force the Japanese Navy had. He could not know that there was not an effective Japanese force that could come down on us from the mainland, behind him, and wipe out the invasion force in his absence. I will always be completely convinced, and I'm sure this is true of Admiral Harry Hill also, completely convinced that his actions were precisely and entirely correct..

After Tinian, we returned to Pearl Harbor to get to work on the next operation which was going to be Iwo Jima.

Q: How closely was Nimitz following the actions on Saipan and Tinian?

Adm. W.: I saw most of the messages and I had the clear impression that he was entirely aware of everything that was going on, just as he was later on, and notably so, in the battle of Leyte Gulf. Personally I saw nothing of an operational nature after Tinian. I was then withdrawn to the Bureau of Ordnance to my great disgust, feeling, of course, by that time that I was an integral and essential part of the war effort! Nevertheless, back to the Bureau of Ordnance I went.

Admiral George Hussey was by that time the chief of the Bureau of Ordnance, Admiral Blandy then being in the Pacific as a task force commander in the amphibious operations.

Q: When you went back to the Bureau what was your particular duty?

Adm. W.: I went back to fire control, and this was a crashing anti-climax for somebody who'd really been concerned directly with the war actively for a long time. I think that George Hussey realized this. Anyway it was so close to the end of the war that almo[st] before I realized what was going on people started telling me, notably Lewis Strauss who was by then a rear admiral, USNR - bette[r] start thinking on how you're going to cancel your contracts, the war is about to be over. This was almost as difficult an operatio[n] as getting the war started. I won't go into all the gory details, but the problem was gargantuan. It wasn't fair to penalize and be so tough with the contractors that they'd go broke. As you probab[ly] recall, they then - and I'm pretty sure still do - operated on a progress payment basis. Otherwise, they don't have enough capital to run the operation. If they suddenly canceled out, there's noth[ing] left but a half-built bunch of steel and other components in the plant, not even enough money to pay for scrapping.

So, the problem was a severe one and it had to be planned for ahead of time. By and large, I think we planned fairly sensibly. There were never to my knowledge or recollection any large court cases or extravagant claims by any contractor that he had been che[at]ed by the government. On the other hand, I don't think the govern[n]ment wasted any unnecessary amounts of money in completing contrac[ts] for material which was not required.

Withington #1 - 81

Q: Approximately how many contractors were involved in your area?

Adm. W.: In my area alone, maybe a couple of hundred, counting subcontractors. Maybe more. But country-wide and defense-wide, thousands.

Q: Practically all the industry in the country was involved?

Adm. W.: Yes. Then the planning was far more important as regards people than it was as regards money or unnecessary material, because they were being thrown out of work by the literally hundreds of thousands. In addition, there was an almost hysterical call from the people "get the boys home," and we demobilized with precipitate haste which we've been paying for ever since, I think, in our relations with the Russians.

Q: That was a lesson that we did not learn from World War I!

Adm. W.: We did even worse after World War II.

Q: Is there any way, in your estimation, that we could have offset this emotional appeal that comes?

Adm. W.: No. The emotions aroused by war have never been more clear than where we are right now with regard to Vietnam, I think. People have a violent revulsion to this thing. In my opinion, frankly, we should never have gotten into it in the first place. They're so unfair that they're not even giving the veteran of Vietnam an even break when he comes home looking for a job or for a better education or a better chance to get ahead. I feel sorry for the kids, particularly the black soldiers, who are not being given an adequate chance today. I'm afraid this is true. Simply because of this revulsion which everybody has now against the war. These kids have done their best. Many of them are blasted and one-armed and one-legged going to veterans' hospitals and nobody gives a darn. Well, I'm sort of digressing from the Bureau of Ordnance at the end of World War II!

I think, on the whole, that the Bureau should be commended historically for the build-up for the war which started in 1939 and then for the wind-down of the war which started in early 1944. It was very difficult to figure out exactly and of course we ended up with large excess quantities, mostly of ammunition. But, aside from that, to my knowledge there was very little egregious waste of anything in the way either of man hours worked or of material that was manufactured and not needed.

Almost before the war ended - I forget the exact date - George Hussey sent for me and said, "I want you to be the commander of the Naval Ordnance Laboratory." This laboratory had been for many years a small activity at the Navy Yard in Washington, the Naval Gun Factory, primarily concerned with the development and production of mines for naval use. They had a brilliant director of mines and other ordnance material in World War II. The mines which General LeMay's airplanes dropped in the Sea of Japan, which throttled the Japanese merchant marine, were all developed at NOL. They had one of the most brilliant stables of civilian scientists, mostly physicists and engineers, that has ever been gathered under one roof, I think, in the United States or anywhere else.

Q: How were they able to assemble them?

Withington #1 - 83

Adm. W.: Well, they got a few good men, and they recruited the others. Most of them worked in civilian clothes. A few like Dr. Ralph Bennett, the technical director, worked in uniform. He had come to the Navy as a Reserve officer from being a professor at MIT.

The Bureau wanted to plan on a large permanent-basis laboratory for their purposes. By the time I arrived on the scene to take over from Captain Schindler, the land at White Oak, just to the east of Silver Spring, had already been purchased. I think something on the order of 1,200 acres, a large tract, partly in Montgomery and partly in Prince George's county. My job was to wind down the laboratory at the end of World War II, attract and organize a permanent staff, keep the laboratory projects going, complete the construction of the large main building and many supporting buildings on the new property, recruit the fire department, and in general prepare for the long term.

Q: Did this mean also the incorporation of knowledge gleaned from the war?

Adm. W.: Yes, trying to boil down the essense of the war experiences.

Q: A gargantuan effort in itself, wasn't it?

Adm. W.: Yes. I think the most interesting challenge was to try to lay a sound basis for the long-term effort of the naval officer commanders and the civilian experts who did the work. We hammered out the charter for NOL, myself and Ralph Bennett, sort of a man with feet in both camps being in a captain's uniform but a physicist himself, and a civilian staff - a charter which George Hussey approved and which later in almost the same words was the charter for the naval ordnance station in China Lake, and other major naval R and D activities. Trying to spell out clearly what the civilian was supposed to do and what the military man was supposed to do, and how they would get along with each other, and what they were supposed to be doing and why.

By the time I was able to get away and go to sea, the admiral moved out to White Oak. There are two nice brick houses out there which were essentially unfinished when I left, but which we had moved into anyhow. Ralph Bennett, the executive director, had one and the Withingtons had the other. This move involved a good many community relations problems with the local people. We accomplished a magnificent public relations coup hiring the initial force for the fire department. Here we were with one foot in Prince George's County and one foot in Montgomery County. From what source should we hire the civilians in the police department? So my genius in the personnel department managed to hire one-third from the District of Columbia, one-third from each of the two counties! I've always thought this was the most perfect public relations coup I've ever heard anything about.

Q: Another element was introduced!

Adm. W.: Yes, and I reported to the local congressmen with the greatest glee that I had done this!

Q: Admiral, you said just a bit ago that part of the job was to make long-range plans to anticipate how the naval officer and the civilian scientist would function together. It occurs to me that perhaps if there was to be a discrepancy in this area, the naval officer, yes, would continue on because he'd been assigned to a certain billet, but the civilian scientist would not be so available in peacetime...

Adm. W.: He could always quit. That's right. So you had hopefully to provide for him a professional opportunity that he couldn't turn down. This was the problem.

Q: How would you do this?

Adm. W.: By seeking for golden words, I guess, and following up words by deeds. When a man was given an assignment, he knew it was his and I didn't interfere with him and neither did any other naval officer.

Q: This involved you with Civil Service, did it not?

Adm. W.: Oh, of course. How did you deal with bureaucracy in that sense?

Adm. W.: Very imperfectly. We had one incompetent man. I think he was a chemist but I don't remember any more. He had Civil Service status and we'd all decided, the military and the council which was all senior civilians, that he had to be fired, and this took literally six months of my time and the senior staff members. We did it. It's very difficult to run a government establishment with Civil Service rules.

Q: Especially in these higher brackets and specialized areas. They didn't have ratings, did they...

Adm. W.: It was a matter of great interest to me, and I think historically. Ralph Bennett, who was a very fine administrator and scientist - incidentally, his particular field, scientifically, was cosmic rays - was the first civil servant ever to get a 10,000 dollar job. I forget what the GS number was. I guess it was 9, but it's not important - no, it was 16. The highest Civil Service rating today is something like 35,000 dollars. The reason this barrier held for so long was that a congressman's salary was only 10,000 dollars and nobody could get more than that, obviously, if he was a government servant. Now, the congressmen get closer to 40,000 dollars, and the senior civil servants are baying hot on their heels!

The NOL period was an exceedingly challenging one as far as people were concerned. We were assigned the Kochel wind tunnel, which had been captured in Germany. And we were also assigned the German scientists and engineers who had worked on the tunnel in Germany.

Q: Were these from Peenemunde?

Adm. W.: Yes, that area. These men arrived from Germany in a prisoner-of-war status about the time that the material was starting to be assembled that had been shipped to this country.

Q: What was their attitude towards participation?

Adm. W.: Surprisingly cooperative. Occasionally we'd have a little Nazi burst from a couple of them, and I wouldn't even bother to talk to the man myself, but I'd have my executive officer do it. I being a little bit versed in protocol by this time! But the men were wonderful. As far as I know all of them are still citizens of the United States. One of them is one of the senior scientists in NASA. Before we left NOL, they ceased to be in prisoner-of-war status, their families came over from Germany. My wife and I went down to Union Station one evening to meet the train that they would come on, standing far back in the background, and the naval officer escort came with these handsome children and shabby, seedy, thin, gaunt-looking women. The women had given everything to the children and kept nothing for themselves. We watched the reunion of these Germans, and sent them down in buses to the old hotel at Indian Head, which was the only place we had for them to live at the moment. And I've never seen happier human faces than those families were when they were collected. As far as I know, they're all good U.S. citizens today, and I feel a great deal of warmth and pride about this.

Q: Tell me about this wind tunnel that you got.

Adm. W.: It had at that time a higher capacity in air speed than anything we had in this country. It was a so-called intermittent tunnel. That is, you evacuated a sphere and that opened the valves, and the air was sucked in past the model, and proper instruments were there to measure the forces on the model. Later on, higher so-called Mach-number tunnels were installed at NOL and elsewhere, and some of continuous blow rather than intermitten blow were designed and built.

Q: Was this very much superior to what the Bureau of Standards had at that time?

Adm. W.: It had a higher capacity at that time - this was 1944 or 1945 - than anything currently in the United States. This, of course, is no longer true. The area of the throat, I think, was 30 or 40 centimeters, so that the size of the models had to be quite small of necessity. But a great deal of important and useful work was done in these tunnels by these men who were, by that time, all civil servants, you see.

Q: How far along had they been in its uses in Germany?

Adm. W.: I believe that the V-1 and V-2 were both developed in that wind tunnel. It did very meaningful service first in Germany, and they hurt the hell out of the British and also the Belgians. They were bombarded with V-1s and V-2s, at Antwerp, as you remember.

The NOL adventure was a great challenge as far as leadership was concerned. We had a big ceremony laying the cornerstone of the main building, and Mr. Forrestal came to do it, and Dr. Tuve, who was the VT fuse developer in World War II, made the keynote speech for us. Oh, he just made the welkin ring. He was wonderful.

That activity has gone forward steadily through the years. I've been on the board of senior citizens which is supposed to advise the Secretary of the Navy on ordnance for the Navy, and I'm a little concerned because the staff is getting a little old and thick between the ears out there. I suppose that should not be printed, but I am. They've all gotten too old, and this is one of the curses of the Civil Service system.

Q: There's no infusion of new blood?

Adm. W.: There is a real conscious effort made to transfer men between stations but it's not enough.

Q: Does this say, in a general way, that the scientific talent of our country is not as readily available in peacetime to our government?

Adm. W.: I'm afraid that it's quite true at NOL and elsewhere that the quality of the staff is sadly inferior to what it was at the end of World War II, when all the best men in the country were available just like that, if they could possibly get away from what they were doing, wherever they were.

Q: Is there possibly another element, too - the fact that in our time now, the military is not terribly popular...

Adm. W.: Oh, this is a tremendous factor, I think.

Q: ...with the intellectual community.

Adm. W.: There are factions, of course, among the scientists and engineers and the good ones are quite as well aware as you or I that this is not a world of peace and roses. If you don't remain armed and ready, you're not going to be alive very long. But many of them are not.

Q: Was this in evidence at all during your time at NOL?

Adm. W.: No. The men there were all quite aware.

Q: How is it possible for a scientific and, so often brilliant, mind to be completely unaware of this other aspect of our ...

Adm. W.: Over-simplifying with just enough intellectual arroganc[e] so that he figures he's an expert in all fields. And he's not, any more than you or I are, not at all. This is an oversimplifica-tion like almost similar comment, but there's a great deal of trut[h] in it. Edward Teller, who's the father of the A-bomb, considers himself to be an expert in all subjects, and he's not. I'm very fond of him, but this is not so. I think Dr. Oppenheimer consider-ed himself to be an expert in all fields. He was very definitely an arrogant man, as well as the most brilliant man, I've ever known by all counts.

I have really cherished the broadening knowledge I gained at NOL in a civilian community, and I've been better for it ever sinc[e] You don't work a laboratory by being a commander, believe me.

Q: It isn't the same as commanding a ship.

Adm. W.: No, it's not the same, not at all.

Q: You've got to be right down in the ranks.

Adm. W.: Oh, yes, you don't command, you persuade, and if a man isn't capable of thinking you can't very well do anything with him by persuading him. There's the old story about looking in the office and seeing a scientist with his head on the table and you don't know whether he's thinking or asleep, do you?

Withington #2 - 92

Interview No. 2 with Rear Admiral Frederic S. Withington, U.S. Navy
(Retired)

Place: His residence in Washington, D.C.

Date: Thursday morning, 17 June 1971

Subject: Biography

By: John T. Mason, Jr.

Q: Good to see you, Admiral. We're going to begin the second chapter by going to sea in January of 1947.

Adm. W.: This was a great event, of course, and my first opportunity to command anything except a shore station. I was ordered to the USS Mississippi which was then in the Navy Yard at Norfolk, Virginia, being prepared as an experimental gunnery and weapons ship to be attached to the Operational Development Force. I was in this fine command for a period of nine months and it was a very happy period for me and my family. Most of our work involved the shooting of guns, since the early evaluation of the Terrier missile program came after my period of command in the Mississippi. We were sort of a pond lily in the sense that we only operated off the Capes, leaving normally on Monday and returning on Friday. The result was that we were used more or less as a receiving ship by the Fleet Personnel people, but they allowed me very kindly to retain a solid core of experienced men both in the officer group and in crew, where we had, I have always thought, a very happy, effective, and efficient group of men running the ship.

Q: Who was in command of OpDevFor at that point?

Withington # 2 - 93

Adm. W.: Admiral Robert R. Briscoe, a great and good friend of mine.

Q: Tell me about some of the things that you tested and used, some of the ordnance.

Adm. W.: We were still concerned with the efficiency of the 5-inch batteries with which the fleet was filled, of course, after World War II, and concerned with methods of finding out how to employ them to better advantage. We used drone airplanes as targets and VT fuses with simply smokepots instead of a high-explosive charge, and the success or failure of the shoot depended on the number of so-called target triggered bursts which occurred. Of course, under the controlled conditions of the shoots, we were certain that the proving ground could do better than the fleet was able to do in actual practice at sea, but we were able, I think, to establish a measure of what the installation should be capable of in expert hands.

Q: It had been installed, and what were some of the bugs that had to be corrected?

Adm. W.: The plotting room on the ship was very extensive, an electrical array of switches, computers, and other machinery. The installation initially was ticklish for the yard people and for the contractors, but we managed to get the systems operating with a minimum of delay and confusion, and we didn't ever, as I recall, run into the installation problem such as the spot from the rangekeeper going in backwards, so that instead of getting to the target you got further away from the target every time you applied the spot.

Fortunately, we didn't run into any such ills as this.

Our most exciting adventure was being able to rescue a young aviator. We were anchored offshore for the night on a very squally, stormy evening, when a young pilot ran out of gasoline and ditched not too far from the ship. He was hurt, but we managed to fish him out and get him back and hoist him aboard, and put him in the sick bay and fill him full of brandy, sew up his cuts, and deliver him safely to his wife the next day. The publicity for the ship and the Navy was very favorable.

Q: Tell me, Sir, why was a battleship used for these experiments?

Adm. W.: The ship was no longer needed as a battleship, as indeed many other battleships were being phased out. The old Wyoming had been this gunnery experimental ship for many years and she just plain wore out, and the Mississippi was a very suitable replacement. She served in this capacity from approximately 1947 through sometime in the late 1950s when she, in turn, wore out, was no longer useful, and was scrapped.

Q: What was the scope of OpDevFor at that point? What other endeavors?

Adm. W.: The scope was approximately what it is today. It included antisubmarine warfare activity at Key West. It included, if I remember correctly, two aviation detachments, one on each coast, which checked all of the aviation ordnance and aviation fire control, which was being developed for the fleet. They worked for the Bureau of Ordnance and the Bureau of Aeronautics, as they still work today for their successors which have different names but very much the same functions.

Q: Do you know, Sir, the origin of this idea - the establishment of OpDevFor? Who conceived of this?

Adm. W.: I'm sorry I can't tell you for sure. I think it was Admiral Willis A. Lee, who was a famous wartime battleship commander and who, before the war, was in the Fleet Training Office in the Navy Department. Admiral J. L. Holloway also may have had something to do with it.

The Operational Development Force was a Navy "first." It was a number of years after that that the Army initiated a similar activity, and after the Air Force separated they set up the activity at Eglin Field in Florida, which is similar in scope and purpose.

Q: It seems like only common sense, an idea of this sort.

Adm. W.: That's right. After the technical services have developed a weapon or weapon system, it is necessary to evaluate it and it should not be necessary for some new ship just going into commission and trying to train the crew and fight the battery and tend the ship - it's unreasonable to expect them to evaluate new equipment. It should be a professional evaluation and, indeed, this is done, in my opinion, superbly well in the Operational Development Force.

Q: In retrospect, if it had been in being at the outset of the war, would we have been able to avoid some of the problems with torpedoes and...

Adm. W.: Yes, I'm quite sure we would. We would have known

immediately that the 1.1 quadruple antiaircraft machine gun mount was inadequate, rather than after it was put to sea in ships which, unfortunately, had to evaluate it unfavorably as well as try to learn how to use it. It was not a good weapon.

Q: This assignment with the <u>Mississippi</u> added to your knowledge, would you say?

Adm. W.: I learned how to handle people, mostly. The knowledge was more important in that respect than technically, although, of course, I learned a great deal in technical matters also.

Q: Would you elaborate on that? It sounds rather intriguing, learning how to handle people.

Adm. W.: You always learn how to handle people when you have to command a ship. This was a postwar Navy when there were very few regulars yet available. I had a fine group of young Reserve officers whose morale had to be considered. They had young wives, and the young wives had problems with which my wife assisted. Probably we did more good for morale among the families ashore than I was able to do on the ship. At any rate, we had a good ship, a good ship's company, and a good ship spirit, and we both worked hard at it.

Q: What sort of complement did the <u>Mississippi</u> have?

Adm. W.: I would say roughly 1,200 officers and men. This is approximate. Not a very large number. We did not have to be ready to steam continuously at sea, of course. We were only taking passage for a matter of hours and not days, anyway. We never went anywhere except out to sea to go to work. She was a very useful ship at that time and I think a quite effective one. I hope so

Q: Were there other units involved at Norfolk simultaneously?

Adm. W.: There were one or two old destroyers, but we very seldom operated together. Once or twice only, I think, during my time. I was actually at sea in the ship perhaps for a period of six months out of my nine months in command. The other three were sweating to get the ship back out of the Navy Yard and finding out whether we could make the machinery run or not, and so on.

From the Mississippi, with Admiral Briscoe's help with the Bureau of Personnel, I was ordered to command the light cruiser Manchester. She was preparing when I arrived in Newport to deploy to the Mediterranean. She was a light cruiser with a 6-inch main battery, a good ship, well trained. I was in command only five months, approximately only for the period of the deployment to the Mediterranean. This was a period when Admiral Forrest Sherman was in command of the Sixth Fleet. He was a strict taskmaster and a very competent naval officer and leader, and it was a great education to work for him. I was a division flagship with my division commander Rear Admiral Eliot Bryant, and while the responsibilities of working for a flag embarked in the ship are not onerous, they can occasionally be perplexing. However, we had the best of mutual relations and I have always felt a great feeling of friendship for him and respect.

This was a fairly quiet period in the Med. The organization included then, as it does now, carriers of the Essex type. It did not include any amphibious-type ships. I believe then, as now, there were a few shore-based airplanes in support of the fleet.

Q: Where were they based?

Adm. W.: I believe in Morocco and Italy. We had more freedom to visit the ports in the Mediterranean then than is possible politically now. For instance, we made the ports in Algeria and Tunis, and this is not politically feasible or done now. We also used Crete, Athens twice. We had a very interesting cruise to the islands of the Aegean Sea, which was more showing the flag and pleasure than professional, but I thoroughly enjoyed it and so did the division commander.

Q: In large measure, that was the purpose, wasn't it?

Adm. W.: Yes, showing the flag.

Q: There was no competition in those days.

Adm. W.: We were aware that the Cold War was going on. It was. It was in full cry. There was no Russian force in the Mediterranean then at all. Nevertheless, we stood a modified war watch when we cruised at night.

Q: Did you go into the Black Sea?

Adm. W.: I did not go there with my ship, and I don't remember that any Sixth Fleet units did, but there wasn't any reason why we shouldn't have done so. There may have been a formal outcry from the Russians, for which they had no right. As you know, the Sixth Fleet still, as a matter of policy, sends a destroyer occasionally into the Black Sea to demonstrate that we have the right to go through the straits.

Q: What repair bases did we use in that time?

Adm. W.: We had no repair bases. Rota now is sort of in a modified way available as a repair base, but it did not exist then nor did the air bases in Spain. We had tenders and oilers with the Sixth Fleet and they were the repair bases. If a ship was in serious difficulty it had to be sent home to a Navy Yard.

Q: Was Valletta available to us?

Adm. W.: I was in Malta with my ship, but Valletta was not very well equipped to handle anything larger than a destroyer or a frigate. I don't know from my own experience whether our ships actually used it for repair purposes or not. The informal headquarters for the Sixth Fleet was the Riviera and of course this is a lovely and beautiful place, and everybody liked it. Those wives who could afford it came out there to be with their husbands. My wife had family concerns in the States and did not come out to the Mediterranean, which we have both always regretted since. This was a very happy period and a very professionally productive period for me.

Q: Was the Royal Navy very much in evidence?

Adm. W.: We saw them, of course, in Malta, otherwise very little. We saw almost nothing of the French. The Russians at that time did not have a Navy which showed any interest in operating outside of home waters. They were not in the Mediterranean at all. The Israelis, the Egyptians, and others were very little in evidence.

Withington #2 - 100

We saw nothing of their ships, as I recall. We did not go to Cairo. We did not go to Israel. In my day in my ship we never moved any farther east than Crete. It was a relatively quiet and stable period in the Mediterranean and, of course, that was the purpose, strategically, of having the fleet there as it hopefully is still today. But the problems are very much more severe for the people who are charged with our responsibilities and commands than they were when I was there.

After this Mediterranean deployment, I returned the ship to Philadelphia to the Navy Yard and was immediately relieved, and then because of my wartime association with Admiral Harry Hill, who was the first president of the National War College, I was fortunate enough to be named to the class of 1949, National War College.

Q: That was the second class, wasn't it?

Adm. W.: That was, I believe, the third class. That's right, yes, and I believe it was Harry Hill's last year as president. This was a great and golden opportunity for all of us and a very happy experience in my life. The class included approximately 120 from the U.S. Navy, Army, Air Force, Marine Corps, a few civilians, one from the Treasury, one from the Bureau of the Budget, and, of course about a third from the State Department. We had three officers each from the services of Canada and Great Britain. These were very valued and esteemed members of the class. Later on, other allied countries put so much pressure on the United States to have students in the college that we had regretfully to terminate the British and Canadian officers included in the school.

Q: The fact that they were present, did this raise any question of security or anything of that sort?

Adm. W.: We never felt uncomfortable either way that I was aware of. We considered that they were one of us. I have a vague recollection that once or twice there was a technical presentation at the college from which they were excluded, but this very seldom, if ever, happened. Nobody ever felt any embarrassment about security whatever.

Q: They were first cousins!

Adm. W.: That's right.

Q: Tell me a little about the course, the lectures, the personnel involved in them.

Adm. W.: The set-up included officers from various services plus visiting professors on loan from universities. The purpose then, and I think it still is, was to broaden the professional attitude and competence of the students. Basically, the course was divided into military and politico-economic parts. I've always felt that for the military, certainly for me, the politico-economic part of the course was the most productive. It was wonderful to sit in the committee with representatives from the State Department and all the services and decide how to fight the next war. This has been going on at the war colleges for many years and, of course, it should.

The more productive effort, I thought, was the overview of all of the intractable foreign relations problems of the United States, all of which are still here in 1971 that we saw in 1948 and 1949, most of which are insoluble. It was the consideration of these problems that I thought was the most interesting and rewarding for the military students at the college.

Q: Much of it would be considered new material for military students, would it not?

Adm. W.: We were learning every day, and of course we learned more from our classmates than we did from our professors, from pooled experience. They still, I know, use the same committee system that we did which changed every month, so that in the course of the nine months of the school year, you were in close association at least once with every one of your classmates, and we were deliberately, by policy, mixed up as to service every time. There was always a chairman of each committee and he was chosen more or less by lot. I don't remember whether I ever was a chairman or not. It wasn't important.

Q: Did you have any one specific paper to present or write?

Adm. W.: We each had a term paper. My subject happened to be the Arabs and Arabian oil which has been an interesting subject for many years and is even more so today.

Q: How did you happen to select that as an area to work in?

Adm. W.: I wanted to learn more about the Arabs and about their religion. I was pretty eager when I started out but became less so. The library facility there is excellent and the library help available is first class.

Q: Who were some of the visiting professors in that day?

Withington #2 - 103

Adm. W.: I'm not sure of the names. I remember a visiting professor of history from Stanford who made the remark that dry farming is always best in wet years, and this has always been a cherished recollection of mine. He was a man with a marvelous sense of humor!

Q: I know how carefully Admiral Hill worked in selecting these visiting professors. This was one of the keystones in the scheme.

Adm. W.: Another cherished recollection is former President Hoover talking to us, and after the lecture - he had not long since finished the Hoover Commission Report - there was a question period as usual and nobody said a word. This was most embarrassing, so Withington finally leaped to his feet and said, "Mr. President, do you think that the Atomic Energy Commission is in the right place in the government structure?" Mr. Hoover looked at me over his glasses and said, "Young man, yes, but don't forget the President has authority to fire anyone on those commissions overnight if he wishes." After that the questions flowed freely.

There was never any sense of pressure at the War College. We were allowed an ample lunch period for athletics. There was soft ball in which Admiral Hill himself participated, there was golf, there was sailing, which was most popular among the Air Force and State Department students for reasons not quite clear to me, bowling, all sorts of activities. There was an occasional evening lecture in which the wives were included. One of them was by the respected historian from Richmond, Douglas Freeman. Another was from Phinney Baxter, then president of Williams College, now retired.

Q: You were right next door to the Industrial War College, were you not?

Adm. W.: That's correct.

Q: Did you have any relationship with them?

Adm. W.: Usually the Industrial College students came in for the morning lecture at the National War College. Not always, but usually. It was they who participated with us, rather than the reverse, and this sort of doubled in brass when the lecture was on the agenda for both colleges, rather than just for the National War College, and it enriched the horizon of the students at the Industrial College, I think.

Q: I'm not exactly clear what the difference is between the two colleges?

Adm. W.: The Industrial College of the Armed Forces is primarily to study the dirty and difficult subject of logistics. How ~~the hell~~ do you get the beans, the bullets, and everything else to the right place at the right time in a war? And this is a subject which is increasingly difficult as arms and armament get more expensive and elaborate and complicated. We'll never be as good at it as we should be. We'll always have to study it, and this is the basic purpose of the Industrial College.

Q: I would think that subject would come into your deliberations at the National War College, too?

Adm. W.: Yes, but only to a lesser extent - never in the depth to which they attempt to study it at the Industrial College. ~~The~~

Q: What was Admiral Hill's role, other than being the chief administrator there?

Adm. W.: He was the sparkplug. He usually himself introduced the speaker every morning, the lecturer, and occasionally he would join in the discussion afterward or ask a question himself of the speaker if he didn't think the students were particularly bright that morning. It was a very bouncy place under Admiral Hill, and a great privilege to be there.

Q: Did Mrs. Hill play a role?

Adm. W.: She worked hard. They lived in one of those beautiful old houses, and her role was entertainment. She worked very hard at it all through the year. There was never a week that they weren't entertaining people, either in droves or in smaller numbers. They were both in good health and both loved the assignment and did exceedingly well at it.

From the War College I eluded the Bureau of Ordnance and managed to obtain orders to the Pentagon, and my sentence there lasted for almost four years.

Q: You say you "eluded" the Bureau of Ordnance because they were after you, weren't they?

Adm. W.: Yes, I was asked for to come back.

Q: What kind of assignment did they have in mind for you?

Adm. W.: I don't remember, but it wasn't very exciting as far as I was concerned, whereas in the Pentagon my opportunity was to be the No. 2 man in the Office of Atomic Energy. This was concerned with nuclear weapons and nuclear power from the standpoint of the Navy. So I was ordered as No. 2, as a captain, under Admiral Tom B. Hill.

Q: How much knowledge did you have of this subject?

Adm. W.: None. I had to pick it all up as I went along.

Q: Well, it was in its infancy, anyway.

Adm. W.: That's right. There was, and I hope there still is, at Sandia Base an orientation course for senior officers. This is a cram course in nuclear physics and it was superbly done in my day. Incidentally, the instructors were all knowledgeable military men. After two weeks of incessant and constant effort, we knew something about the basics of nuclear physics, and, of course, this is the foundation stone for the weaponry and for nuclear power.

Q: This was at Sandia?

Adm. W.: Sandia Base, yes, and it was part of the preparation for getting into the job.

Q: Was Hayward involved in that?

Adm. W.: Yes, he was. There were then a number, as you know, of very able military officers from all three services concerned with what was then called the Armed Forces Special Weapons Project. It is now called DASA, I think, but it has the same purposes.

Q: At the end of the decade of the forties, which was this time, wha was the objective in the use of atomic energy? What was the philosophy prevailing at that moment?

Adm. W.: The relationship between the Atomic Energy Commission and the military was through a committee, the Military Liaison Committee, and in my time it had a civilian chairman, two civilian chairmen. Occasionally it has had a retired military officer, but I think, on the whole, it has continued to this day to have a civilian chairman. This committee is the go-between between the Atomic Energy Commission and the military services. The budget for weapons, including nuclear material, for the military is in the AEC budget, and this is a very interesting set-up because the amount of money involved through the years has been many billions of dollars, both in the actual nuclear material and weaponry and in the facilities to make it.

In effect, we have hidden enormous military costs in a civilian budget picture in AEC, and this reduces the military budget, but nevertheless it's a military cost.

Q: This is a deliberate...?

Adm. W.: I don't exactly know why the bookkeeping was set up this way at the start, but it was and it has so continued. We criticize the Russians for hiding their military expenditures all through their budget, yet here we are in a major fashion doing the same thing ourselves.

Q: Does the Congress ever raise an eyebrow over this?

Adm. W.: As you know, one of the most effective of the congressional committees is the Joint Committee on Atomic Energy. It always has been, historically. They know all about this, but apparently they don't object to it. They understand it thoroughly. In fact, some of those men are more knowledgeable about the whole field, in my opinion, than some of the commissioners on the AEC itself.

Q: And from the viewpoint of a casual observer, they are some of the less loquacious members of Congress.

Adm. W.: That's correct, and I'm not aware ever of a breach of security having occurred in that connection, as far as the committee staff either.

Q: Who were some of the members you dealt with at that time?

Adm. W.: I'm trying to remember. Scoop Jackson, who was then a young senator, was one of them.

Q: Was Holifield there then?

Adm. W.: Yes. My own personal relationships with Congress at that time were very minimal. I was just aware that these men were there. I never had to appear at a hearing of the Joint Committee. Our area of negotiation was between the Pentagon and the AEC headquarters, and sometimes these negotiations were very delicate, particularly since the Navy and the Air Force were - not frequently, but occasionally - in sharp disagreement on what size of weapons should be developed for air delivery. The Air Force generally at that time favored larger weapons than the Navy did. They have since been proved wrong, but this is of little importance.

The interesting part at the time was the sometimes homeric battles

Withington # 2 - 109

that occurred behind the scenes.

Q: Was there any change in the direction of your endeavors after Eisenhower came to the presidency and expounded "atoms for peace" as a policy?

Adm. W.: No. I'm a little bit uncertain about the sequence of the presidency relative to my own time in office. I relieved Tom Hill as the head of this office of Naval Atomic Energy after about a year, and he left and went to sea. I was thereafter one of the two Navy members on the Military Liaison Committee, and so quite aware of the difficulties and the intricacies of some of the intercommunication between the military and the civilians.

At that time, there was a very important activity run by military officers in the Commission called the Military Applications Division. It was so-called then, and I believe it still is. This division under military leadership, one of whom was Admiral Jim Russell in my time, had actually to spend most of the money appropriated to the Commission. What they didn't spend Admiral Rickover and the Reactor Development Division did!

In Op-36 we were concerned at that time, in the early days of nuclear power. The first water-moderated reactor was being developed under Westinghouse, the first liquid-metal reactor was being developed by the General Electric Company at a place called West Milton, near Schenectady. The reactor test facility at Arco in Idaho was then being undertaken. It was a very exciting period in the development of nuclear power in this country, and I was very interested and fascinated to be in it. Relationships with Rickover, at the time, were cordial, but, shall I say, formal. The man is a very prickly individual, very able, very sure always that he's right and, of course he's not always right. We managed to get along without any serious amount of friction.

Q: But you did deal with him?

Adm. W.: Oh, yes.

Q: At a little later day, I was told, things had come to such a pass that he was never included in discussions on atomic energy within the Navy.

Adm. W.: I'm sure that's correct, but it was not true in my day. At least, personally, as between Withington and Rickover, there was never any serious problem.

Q: How much did you have to do with Admiral Strauss?

Adm. W.: He was and is a cherished and dear old friend. I had to deal with him, and also with his predecessor chairman Gordon Deane of whom I was very fond. I was also very fond of Dr. Larry Hafsta who was head of the reactor development division, and later left government service to be director of research for General Motors, and is now retired.

As far as personal development was concerned, this was a grea period for me. I met the leading scientists of the day, including Dr. Robert Oppenheimer, who was the most brilliant man by all odds I've ever known.

When Tom Hill went to sea in 1949, I was promoted to Rear Admiral and relieved him.

Q: That was before the cloud descended on Oppenheimer?

Adm. W.: Yes. I met Dr. Edward Teller. The names are not readily available to me in retrospect, but the impact of contact with these minds is still with me. We would visit, among many other places, the radiation laboratory at Berkeley which is still there. We saw the various accelerators then in operation or in development. We talked with the director of the laboratory. We talked with his brilliant scientists, one of whom was concerned with the riddle of life, how does energy from the sun get into food? Much, of course, is known about this in theory but very little in actual practice, and these brilliant men were concerned with really the basics of how we live and why.

Q: Government monies were going into some of these laboratories, were they?

Adm. W.: Yes. The University of California was the contractor to the Commission for the radiation laboratory, also for the Los Alamos scientific laboratory in New Mexico, and, later, for the new laboratory, after my day, at Livermore, California. It was, and is, a little unclear to me why we have to keep right on firing nuclear test shots. It seems to me that we should long since have learned almost all there is to know about the use of nuclear fission in weapons, but apparently this is not so.

There also seems to be an insatiable appetite for weapons effects tests. This, fortunately, has been aborted by the agreement with the Russians to cease atmospheric testing. You can't strew the desert with old tanks, guns, airplanes, and similar objects, and subject them to atomic tests if you're forbidden to shoot in the air. But for many years we did this thing, starting with the first major experiment with ships and equipment of all kinds at Bikini atoll right after World War II and the first atomic bomb explosions.

This was a very early and productive period in the investigation of the atom. At that time, the effort to develop a reactor which would breed, that, is, would produce more thermonuclear material than it would consume, was already begun. We had hopes then that it would soon bear fruit and it has not still, today, borne fruit. The problem, as I recall, was basically one of the extreme difficulty of containing the working fluid because of corrosion, and I believe this is still the basic problem in all similar attempts. I'm sure it's going to be solved some day, just as I have faith that we'll some day have thermonuclear power from the sea, but we don't know how to do this yet. Incidentally and very interestingly, as far as I know, we have complete exchange on a nonclassified level with the Russians on attempts to develop thermonuclear power. Both of us obviously know how to use this power in weapons, so this is irrelevant and beside the point, but neither of us knows how to contain the energy long enough to obtain useful power.

Q: Admiral, coming down to the present for a moment, has there been any setback in the development of some of these things because of the cut-off of federal funds to universities and colleges?

Adm. W.: I'm not in any position to know about that. My own feeling is that some of the cut-offs to colleges have simply cut off boondoggles. A good deal of the work in the colleges has not been very important for the military or, indeed, for the country. As you know, the Office of Naval Research did start as a pioneer investing government research and development money into the universities, and they did this exceedingly well, I think - guiding without holding a whip over the contractors. Now, under the National Science Foundation, the whole picture is much more elaborate and complex. I'm not sure the results are any better, if as good. There was a great deal of clamor about the lapse in government support of research and development as opposed to the Russians. In the first place, I don't think we know very clearly how much the Russians do spend because they certainly aren't going to tell us. In the second place, I'm not at all sure that some tightening up isn't clearly in order.

The big money, of course, doesn't go into the laboratories. It goes into the purchase of things like the SST prototypes at a couple of billion dollars each, this is part of the R and D load and all programs for weapons, indeed, for anything that is mechanical, electrical, flies, soars, or what-have-you.

Q: During your regime there what was the state of missile development?

Adm. W.: There was no concern at this period for missile warheads. We didn't have any missiles that required warheads. That came much later.

Q: Did we anticipate them?

Adm. W.: Only in a very vague sort of way. There was no actual development work then in progress that I knew of, and I would have known.

Q: We had the background in rocketry with Professor Goddard.

Adm. W.: Yes. Of course, we had the rocket background - successful background - of World War II. There was a program of missiles in its infancy, but far too infant to be of any concern, at least at the Navy level, my level, for nuclear warheads.

Q: So that implies that Polaris was not really on the drawing boards

Adm. W.: That's correct.

I think that this may be enough for this tour of duty in the Pentagon. It lasted for upwards of four years and after having lived for four years in the District and fought the battle of the bridges, which was even then very bad, twice a day every working day, I was glad to leave the Pentagon and go to sea.

Q: Would you tell me something first, before leaving that era, about the problems of getting the basic mineral supplies?

Adm. W.: The raw materials?

Q: Yes.

Adm. W.: At that time, the most important supplier was the Belgian Congo, and we had a nice comfortable relationship with the Belgian government so that, in effect, we monopolized the whole production. This was the richest then-known source of uranium ore. There was also an agreement by which the British had a certain percentage of this ore.

There was a good deal of effort in the West looking for uranium but at that time - and I think since - we never found as rich a source of ore as the Katanga source was in the Congo. I don't know whether this Belgian source is still in force or not. It isn't any of my business to know. Since that time, large and important sources of uranium have opened up in Canada, which have been available to us as well as to the Canadians and the British.

The Russians have their own sources which appear to be ample. We do know, however, that the amount of uranium in the earth which is obtainable and usable is very limited and that we had better get on with the business of breeding or we're going to run out of material in another fifty to seventy-five years, or something like this. Oil is going to run out and natural gas from the oil deposits is going to run out. Some day, even coal will run out, then we're left with oil shale and with the problem that must be solved of obtaining power from sea water, thermonuclear power.

Q: Or maybe the sun?

Adm. W.: Maybe the sun, but this is too difficult, I think.

Q: What sort of cooperation did we give in your regime to the British?

Adm. W.: Relationships were not close. The Brian McMahon Act strictly limited the interchange between ourselves and the British and the Canadians. I, of course, had no direct responsibility at all, but I was aware that matters were difficult and, indeed, they have continued as difficult to this day because the law has never been changed, the Atomic Energy Act.

Q: And one more item, Sir: in that time, a policy of the utmost secrecy prevailed, it seems to me, in every area of the atomic energy effort. That is not so now. Why the contrast, why the change?

Adm. W.: The basic answer is that there was then nuclear scarcity and there's now nuclear plenty. I'm sure this is the right answer. Indeed, in my day there was a school of thought to which I subscribed that we ought to print every day at the masthead of <u>The New York Times</u> the number of weapons that we had then available in the stockpile. Why not? The Russians had a pretty good idea of the number anyway, and why not give some comfort to our own people? This, of course, has never been done and it's not done now. We know now that there are a good many thousands of these weapons in all kinds of forms and shapes.

Q: That very same idea, is that not perhaps at back of the idea of the need to test weapons under the earth, above the earth, and in every fashion - telling the enemy that we have them in use?

Adm. W.: The propaganda part of this thing is undoubtedly a large factor, yes. It's a very interesting game. I've not attempted to keep up with the advances in nuclear physics, the continuing discovery of new nuclear particles inside the nucleus of the atom. The ultimate glue that keeps the atom together is still undiscovered, I believe, although the large machines have discovered some fifty particles, or bits of matter, of smaller magnitude than the proton, the neutron, and the electron, which used to be the three building blocks in my day.

Q: And they were considered the ultimate, weren't they?

Adm. W.: Yes, that's right. They still exist, of course, but there are many things inside of them which we know now but we didn't know then. Life was simpler in those days.

Withington #2 - 117

Q: Did you, coming relatively fresh to this whole picture, have a considerable amount of homework to do in these years?

Adm. W.: Maybe I should have, but I didn't. There was plenty of time in the office to study a paper. We were not involved too strenuously in interservice wars in those days and there was time to look at the data from the AEC on physics, on experiments at Sandia, on the work at Los Alamos, and we learned a great deal from working during office hours. You couldn't take the mass of material home anyway because of its classification. We had to work on it in the office.

Q: What sort of encouragement and support did you receive from men like Fechteler and Carney?

Adm. W.: This was very interesting. Knowledge of nuclear matters was very meager in the Navy at that time at the higher level and I undertook, with the blessing of the CNO, to teach a little class on the basics, and one of the vice admirals whom I shall not name called me in afterwards and said, "Who the hell are you to be telling us about this?" He didn't appreciate that any effort was necessary on the part of senior officers to understand this subject at all. This was not a general attitude, though.

Q: It wasn't obligatory for them to attend?

Adm. W.: No. "Who the hell are you"! That was quite a shock! I was merely trying to be helpful.

Q: It really takes a while for appreciation of a new subject to percolate though.

Withington #2 - 118

Adm. W.: The testing of weapons was going on in my day and I was one of the observers at the Eniwetok atoll to see the first thermonuclear explosion. This series of experiments at Eniwetok involved exposure not only of material to the blast and thermal and nuclear effects, but also of animals, and they were so meticulou about the animals that the scientists insisted that they be ~~grabbed~~ bred on the spot, on the island, and the Commission forked out a lot of good money to build animal runs for pigs and dogs and rats on one of the islands of the atoll. A great emergency arose. The pigs were unable to copulate because the cement in the enclosures was too slippery so the enclosures had to be modified in order to breed piglets.

Q: Make them abrasive!

Adm. W.: This is a true story! The dogs, unfortunately, were a particularly appealing breed of hunting dogs from the mountains of Tennessee, and it just hurt everybody to use them for this purpose.

Q: Was there any apparent lack of fertility in these animals?

Adm. W.: I think not. No trouble! This was before, of course, they were exposed to the blast and heat.

Q: For this series of tests at Eniwetok, we did entertain all sorts of foreign observers, did we not?

Adm. W.: No. This was Bikini, earlier. By the time of Eniwetok we were not inviting any foreigners. There were none, I'm sure, when I was out there.

Q: Was this not also the time when there was a great deal of publicity on the dangers of fallout?

Adm. W.: This came a little later on, when we, unfortunately, irradiated the crew of a Japanese fishing boat. This was after my day. Of course, there was great concern about where the cloud was going to go and the tests had to be set when the wind was from the proper direction, or it would be postponed. The fact that there was death in this cloud was well known at the time, of course.

Q: But were the scientists as fearful of the results as was the press?

Adm. W.: No. They were more, not certain, but confident that their predictions would be correct, that there would only be a certain amount of this stuff, that it would go in the right direction if we just did it the right day, and that by the time the particles started to fall out many thousands of miles and hours later, the worst of the nuclear debris from the explosion would have lost its potency through the laws of physics and the way the half life works in the various substances and the isotopes.

The nuclear period ended when I went to sea as an amphibious group commander in the Pacific. This was a period of about a year. I was delighted to be out of the bureaucratic mazes of Washington. Actually, the flagship was in Far Eastern waters when I took over the command and was back there again a year later when I was relieved. In between I took the first contingent of Navy ships to the Arctic for the basic supply of the so-called DEW lines on the northern shores of Canada and Alaska. This, of course, of necessity had to be a midsummer operation with hopefully a minimum of Arctic ice and ice packs. We hit a rather bad year. The flagship came within two feet of being stranded one night by the ice pack just off Point Barrow. I was afraid - we all were - from the time we got into the ice until we got out of it. I had a lot of intrepid people in the LSTs, the tugs, and the smaller ships with me. They did manage to push their way along the coast from Barrow eastward to the bases which had been selected for the various radar station with the equipment, delivered it, and returned. The message I sen which gave me more satisfaction than any other in my whole life in the Navy was, "All ice astern" after leaving Point Barrow.

We had some significant damage to ships, most to propellers, but we had some intrepid Navy divers who worked from the tug in this cold 30-degree-temperature water. We had spare propellers an they actually changed a few propellers on the smaller ships.

Q: That must have been quite a feat in that cold water.

Adm. W.: Oh, it was a great feat. These were some of the bravest men I've ever seen in my life.

Q: I thought the physical endurance was limited to minutes.

Adm. W.: That's right. That was another one of their good effort They had the very best available in the way of equipment and suits but even so there was no protection against the cold.

We didn't lose any ships, we did deliver the material, and we were damned lucky, and I never want to go back to the Arctic again, thank you very much.

Q: Was that your first introduction?

Adm. W.: First and last.

Q: These radar stations were a part of our line of defense, weren't they?

Adm. W.: That's right. They were supposed to give early warning – Distant Early Warning is what DEW means – against attack by airplanes. Of course, the Russians never intended to attack by airplane over the pole, and I don't believe these stations are of any real value against missiles. But perhaps they are. I don't know how much has been done to modernize the installation since this time, which was 1953.

Q: Were there any repercussions at that point from Canada that we were using her territory to establish our own defenses?

Adm. W.: This was with the entire collaboration of Canada. One or two of their ice experts were on my ship to help predict the movement of ice. We had complete cooperation from the Canadians throughout.

Q: In more recent years countries have been shy of the installation of defenses against atomic attack ...

Adm. W.: I don't remember whether any of these stations went as far east as Canada or not. Very likely they didn't. All of them were on the north coast of Alaska. I believe this was the case, but we had complete cooperation from the Canadians at all times.

Q: Did you have any disturbance of your communications from one ship to another?

Adm. W.: Yes, there are complete communication blackouts between

Withington #2 - 12

Arctic waters and the rest of the world. I believe this is also true from the Antarctic, but I don't know for sure. The aurora borealis and its peculiarities seem to be part of this blackout. Whether the problem has been corrected today or not, I don't know. We found ourselves repeatedly for a matter of hours completely isolated from the world with no communication either in or out.

Q: That was rather unique for a naval force, wasn't it?

Adm. W.: It may be unique, but it was well known to be a fact and had been for years.

Q: This stems, you say, from the aurora borealis ...

Adm. W.: That is a part of it, but I don't think it's the whole answer. I don't know what the whole answer is, and I don't think anybody else does either. There are various layers above the eart atmosphere, the ionsphere, and many other spheres. These are all involved in this phenomenon, why I don't understand.

Q: Obviously the personnel of your ships on an expedition like that have to have a fairly complete life. What sort of amusement was provided for them?

Adm. W: The whole thing didn't take very long. We had only the usual things on the ships. I had one of the command ships, the Es We had the usual movies and other sorts of amusement. The LSTs had very meager sources of amusement on board, but of course they had movies. We had two cargo ships, as I remember it. The amusement the battle to survive in the ice. We had, of course, an icebreake This happened to be the Coast Guard's <u>Northwind</u> with one of the mo intrepid men I've ever known in command. He was a tower of streng throughout.

Q: Who was he?

Adm. W.: I don't remember his name.

The Russians, I believe, even then had better icebreakers than we did and I believe they still do. As you know, they maintain a sufficient force of icebreakers to use the northern passage around Asia in summertime, and I believe their knowledge of the weather and their use of icebreakers has been so effective that they gradually extended the period of the year when they could use this northern route for military ships and for merchant ships.

Q: I know that during World War II we were a great source of supply for them for icebreakers.

Adm. W.: I think they're better technically at building icebreakers today than we are.

During these two deployments in the Far East the Korean War was still winding down. Negotiations were interminably going on at Panmunjon without success, men were still dying across from the parallel where the armistice line is today. The Navy was concerned with support of the Army in Korea. We had many more troops there then than the 50,000 which are still involved. There was the United Nations command under U.S. command with significant British, Turkish, Thai, and other national units. It was, at least on paper, a completely international force. Actually, of course, the strength of it was in U.S. troops and in the ROK, the Korean troops. We had landing exercises with Army units in the vicinity of Seoul. I visited the front lines. We were in Japan several times, where again my old friend Admiral Briscoe was stationed, this time as commander of Naval Forces, Far East.

I made it my business while I was there to call upon Admiral Nomura, who was ~~then~~ the ambassador in Washington at the time of Pearl Harbor.

Q: The one-eyed chap?

Adm. W.: That's right. He became a very close friend. He was a man whom I admired greatly. He told me at that time, and I've no reason to doubt his word, that nobody told him from Japan what was going to happen when he was ambassador here..

Q: This he told you when you were in the Far East?

Adm. W.: Yes.

Q: You knew him in Washington?

Adm. W.: No, I had never known him. As I say, I made a point to seek him out in Japan when I was there in 1953. One of the nice things that happened - he had been for many years a member of the Naval Institute and after the war the then Secretary-Treasurer, whose name I don't know, took the trouble to gather up all the back numbers which he had missed and send them to him. This was one of the things that pleased him more than anything else postwar that ever happened. A little item of incidental information, but it was an important thing to do for our relations with Japan. The old man was until his death a very large factor as an adviser to the government. He had no responsibility of his own. He had some more or less honorary business connections which gave him a comfortable living, but nothing more than comfortable. He broadcast in English in 1959 on the 4th of July a message of friendship to the United States on the radio. He believed firmly that the interests of Japan coincided, at that time, with the interests of the United States. He told me once that always the interests of Japan would coincide with our interests and vice versa. I looked at him over my glasses and said, "Admiral, do you really believe that?" He laughed, and after that we understood each other much better!

Q: I take it his status was different from the status of many other high ranking naval officers in postwar Japan.

Adm. W.: He was never considered to have been a criminal in any way. I'm not sure that that whole effort wasn't very much misguided, in retrospect. At any rate, it's done and irreversible now. We're feeling some of the effects of it in Vietnam, I feel sure - the effects of our purges both in Japan and in Germany.

Q: Tell me more about the Korean operation.

Adm. W.: We knew very little of it, really. We were simply able with our small number of ships to provide some drill for some of these Marines who were not in the line at the time.

Q: This was post-Inchon?

Adm. W.: Oh, yes, this was 1953. The Korean War was officially over, but the armistice negotiation was still in process and men were still dying. In fact, while we were in port we could see the hospital ship and the casualties being flown in by helicopter.

Q: You said you got to Seoul?

Adm. W.: Yes.

Q: Did you have any contact with Sygman Rhee?

Adm. W.: We called on the old man, later, in 1958. He was then very old, and it had to be carefully arranged so that he'd be awake and aware when you were there. He was interesting, and, of course, he did all the talking. I did all the listening!

Q: The over-all command was in the hands of Admiral Radford on the naval side, was it not?

Adm. W.: The command business is always difficult in both the NATO and in the Pacific. The commander, Naval Forces, Far East, was Admiral Briscoe. He reported, I think, both to the UN commander who was an Army general, General Mark Clark, and to CinCPac. I don't remember who was CinCPac at that time. It was always a pretty confused situation, and you always wondered who was the boss. Anyway, I knew who my boss was when I was out there - that was Admiral Briscoe. There was never any doubt about it.

The other major item in that year was a full division landing exercise at Camp Pendleton. This was lots of fun. We had aircraft carriers and a slew of transports, LSTs, LVTs. Having been in the amphibious forces in World War II, of course I figured I knew something about this, and I think we carried out the exercise pretty successfully, though with obviously many artificialities. It was a pretty successful landing.

Q: Were there any contrasts with World War II in techniques?

Adm. W.: We had the same material. No. The techniques were the same, except for the use of helicopters which we had then which were not available, of course, in World War II. These were the early days of their use. As I remember, we didn't have any fatal casualties. I don't remember that we had any fatal accidents in the landing, which was highly unusual. We had good luck with the weather.

Q: This new dimension, was it a useful one?

Adm. W.: We attempted to simulate the use of atomic bombs. We knew there weren't any going to fall but with me as the attack force commander — the landing force commander was a Marine Corps general — the threat doesn't have any reality. But of course, it is a real threat and the simulated drops would have wiped out the landing force, as it turned out.

Q: How big a landing force was it?

Adm. W.: I can't tell you how many ships...

Q: How many men?

Adm. W.: We were attempting to land the greater part of a Marine division. We did land them. But the ships offshore would have been cruelly — I wouldn't say decimated because that means only a tenth destroyed, and much more than ten percent of the ships offshore would have been destroyed by the simulated drop if it had actually occurred. As a matter of fact, the drop practically went down the stack of my command ship.

Q: That reference to a simulated atomic bomb leads me to the thought that this was in the period when the United States had proclaimed the doctrine of massive retaliation as a means of defending itself. Was this a valid doctrine to have proclaimed? Were we prepared to implement it?

Adm. W.: This would have been implemented by the Strategic Air Command. It was before the days when, as a matter of course, all of the naval aircraft carriers were prepared to drop nuclear weapons with warheads. Yes, the Strategic Air Command could certainly have taken off and wiped out the Russian cities. Thank heaven, they didn't.

Q: Would we actually have done it, if tempted, do you think?

Adm. W.: It's impossible to say, but I don't believe so, no.

Q: The reaction to the mere suggestion on MacArthur's part that atomic weapons be used in Korea was rather strenuous.

Adm. W.: Yes, it was, and the British prime minister came flying to Washington. All hell broke loose.

Q: Did you say you made two trips to the Far East?

Adm. W.: Yes. It was about this period, I think, that Dr. Oppenheimer made his remark about the two scorpions in the bottle, relative to nuclear weapons and the United States and Russia. There's not much point in the two scorpions fighting since they'd both obviously end up dead. Unfortunately, in modern days with other countries either equipped with nuclear weapons in small numbers or able, on rather short order, to equip themselves there are more than two scorpions, so that the situation is more complex than it was in Oppenheimer's day. I still hope that we'll never - we or our children or our grandchildren - see a nuclear weapon used in war, in anger. But anything is possible. It's horrible and frightening to contemplate.

Q: This conviction on your part is born of close association.

Adm. W.: I have seen those test explosions. Incidentally and most interestingly, the only actual use of a nuclear weapon completely simulated, including the detonation, which has ever taken place was the firing of a Polaris missile in the Pacific. This was done fairly early in the Raborn program and I can't imagine how we ever got permission from all of the civilian authorities in the United States to do it, but it was done. The Air Force has never been allowed to do this. They've never made a full-scale simulation, including thermonuclear explosion. Of course, they've dropped many test bombs.

Many people say that the whole full-scale test is not necessary since you can assume that the weapon will go off, that it's infallible. But nothing is infallible in the way of ordnance. This is the only thing I'm quite sure of from my long experience. It's a comfort to everyone to know that the damned thing did go off at the end of the 1,200 miles or whatever its range was.

Q: Wasn't this assumption at the root of our problem with torpedoes at the outset of World War II?

Adm. W.: Yes.

Q: That we had assumed that...

Adm. W.: The warhead would work. The warhead was perfect and it was no good at all.

The end of my all-too-brief sea duty came with a rather cold slap in the face. There was no job for me so I was ordered to the Naval War College as a special class of one under instruction. I came home to Washington on leave and, while on leave, the telephone rang and the detail officer said, "Don't do anything. Hold everything. Don't make any Newport arrangements. Admiral Deke Parsons has just died at the Naval Hospital, Bethesda, and you're going to be his relief," he then being the deputy chief of the Bureau of Ordnance.

Q: Was this actually what they had in mind for you, anyway?

Adm. W.: No, I don't think so.

Q: Why were you then called back from the amphibious command?

Adm. W.: Oh, the sea duties were so precious that my time was up. I had to go, no matter whether there was any place to send me ashore or not. Of course, I would have very happily stayed on but this was not permitted.

Q: What did they contemplate for you at the Naval War College? What kind of a study were you going to undertake?

Adm. W.: A senior course under instruction. I was pretty vague about it. I don't know what the thought was, but the whole idea had no appeal for me and I'm glad it didn't come off. After the National War College I figured I'd had enough of senior instruction. I wanted to do more work and less study.

Withington #2 - 131

Q: There comes a time when you have to stop going to school!

Adm. W.: Yes, that's right. Admiral Parsons was the bombardeer at Hiroshima, one of the gentlest and kindest men I've ever known and also one of the ablest. He was the first true scientist in uniform. He worked throughout the period of the Manhattan Project as assistant to Dr. Oppenheimer at Los Alamos. He had a very fine theoretical mind. He wasn't as good a tactical line officer as many of his contemporaries, but, nobody can have everything.

Q: What was his first name, actually?

Adm. W.: William S. Parsons. After his sudden and regrettable early death, I was called in to relieve him and I found in the bottom right-hand drawer of his desk a container of 500 aspirin tablets, mostly unused, so during my period as his successor until I took over as chief, I was the owner of the aspirin tablets.

Q: Continued unused?

Adm. W.: I used them occasionally.

Q: Just a bit of digression. Tell me - you said he wasn't the greatest line officer. Is this not a commentary on the system of promotions as it was, that a man had to have frequent duties at sea in order to achieve an increase in rank, even though he was a specialist in various areas?

Adm. W.: We discussed this, I know, last time. There is undoubtedly a happy medium between the rigid requirement that everybody has to command a ship and the abolition of such a requirement and the possibility that a man may never go to sea at all and still become an admiral. I don't know what this happy medium should be

Q: Well, as you evaluate your own development and your own caree what would you say about your frequent sea duty as an asset?

Adm. W.: I would never have been an effective naval officer with out it. I was probably low on the sea duty side for developing a naval officer of complete all-around ability. For instance, I only had one year out of all my youthful years with any engineering duty at all. All the rest was with gunnery. This is not a very good balance. I was only navigator for a period of less tha a year in a destroyer.

Q: Wouldn't it be possible to plan more carefully a man's career and give him the proper kind of assignments, rather than indiscriminate ones?

Adm. W.: Career-planning is, of course, done in the Bureau of Naval Personnel. Nobody is ever satisfied with it for himself or for what he thinks he sees in others. There has always been a gre and almost, at times, convulsive effort to make sure that everybod got a fair break and a rounded education as a naval officer. I'm sure this is true today. The concept of what a well-rounded caree should include is a matter of vigorous disagreement often. The Bureau thinks something different from the individual and vice ver The problem will never be settled to anybody's satisfaction. It will always be attacked with a lot of good will, a lot of determir ation, and a lot of effort. I don't think on the whole we've done too badly through the years, but it's inherently insoluble. And t needs of the Navy change as the years go on. They change very much. There's a necessity for high-level infighting in the Pentagon with the other departments - military departments - and with the Secretary of Defense and his enormous bureaucracy, which did not exist in my day. You have to develop officers with proper career experience who can be promoted into those jobs and handle themselves well and do the Navy some good. So you have too many variables there to come up with any nice pat solution of this problem, and the variables keep changing!

The chief of bureau when I took over as assistant chief was Admiral M. F. Schoeffel, a naval aviator. He was an old friend and our relationship from the start was exceedingly cordial. There was, at that time and continued in my time as chief, some very vigorous rivalry between the Bureau of Ordnance and the Bureau of Aeronautics. This was particularly true in the field of missiles and it did the Navy no good. We had a group of highly dedicated and able naval aviators on duty in the Bureau of Ordnance. There was an equally dedicated and able group in the Bureau of Aeronautics, and they fought sometimes like cats and dogs. It was just purely and simply disgraceful.

Q: Was it intended to offset that rivalry to have, for instance, Schoeffel as head of the...

Adm. W.: That was the hope, yes. But the inter-bureau rivalries continued to flourish. The chiefs in his day and also in mine had the best of personal relationships, but no matter what we said the troops did differently.

Q: Why this parochialism? Why the inability to see the whole picture?

Adm. W.: I don't know. It's profoundly depressing. There was a question of "cognizance." This was a dirty word, but it also existed between the Bureau of Ordnance and the Bureau of Ships. What part of the turret belonged to the Bureau of Ships and what part to the Bureau of Ordnance? What part of a gun mount? What part of a missile-launcher, etc., etc?

Q: My empire and yours!

Adm. W.: My empire and your empire. Not invented here. All of these dreadful phrases. One of the direct sources of dispute in the Bureau of Aeronautics was cognizance over bomb racks. Bomb racks, of course, are an integral part of the airplane, yet if they don't fit the bomb they're not worth a dam. Who should be responsible?

Q: I should think that in itself would teach cooperation.

Adm. W.: Well, it just caused discord!

Q: Did you, being catapulted into this job as assistant, did you have any course of orientation?

Adm. W.: There wasn't any time. Of course, I had been orientated, so to speak, for many years in NOL and in the Bureau of Ordnance itself and in the Pentagon, so I knew what the score was. There wasn't anybody who could teach me, really. It was too late!

Q: You were too bright anyway.

Adm. W.: No, that had nothing to do with it. At that point, it was much too late to send me to school anywhere.

I might refer again to that school at Sandia Base in nuclear physics. That was the most effective cram course I've ever seen for a senior officer, and I hope it's continuing. I don't know.

Q: And who organized that?

Adm. W.: The Armed Forces Special Weapons Project, now called DASA. That's the same outfit. The organization which is responsible for the nuclear weaponry of the services.

Q: Since it was a cram course, it must have called for a large capacity on the part of the participants.

Adm. W.: It required total concentration, yes, or you got nothing out of the course.

Going back to those days, I might mention that there was at Kirkland Field at Albuquerque a small naval unit whose duty was to ensure that the nuclear weapons being developed for the services could be flown in naval airplanes, and this was one of the places where the fabulous Chick Hayward was concerned. He commanded this unit at one time.

A little anecdote about Hayward illustrates the quirky nature of the man's mind. He was flying Admiral Sherman, then the Chief of Naval Operations, from Albuquerque to San Diego in an A.J. airplane. This plane had two propeller engines and a jet in the tail. While Admiral Sherman was flying this - of course, he was a naval aviator, too - Hayward, without telling him, cut off both of the propeller-type engines and there he was flying the plane on the jet! This also is a true story. I think that Sherman was not pleased.

Q: Probably didn't faze Hayward at all!

Adm. W.: Oh, no.

I have made a considerable effort, going through the papers, to look for individual subjects of interest during this long period in the Navy Department, which was from 1954 to 1958. I have very few direct recollections of individual events. After I took over as the chief, Captain Hooper arrived to be the head of the research division and recommended and I approved a thorough reorganization of the Bureau's efforts. Hooper was and is an exceedingly able man who, as you know, is now the director of naval history. His ideas were good. The senior civilians were all for it and worked hard for it, as well as the officers in the department, and the research efforts of the Bureau were better directed and guided from that time on, I'm sure.

What has happened in recent days, with the many reorganizations at upper levels in the research and development arena, I don't know. I just hope that things are going reasonably well.

Q: Would you begin, perhaps, by giving me the scope of your activities as assistant and then lead into the other?

Adm. W.: The assistant, of course, is what the chief wants him to be, what he thinks the chief wants him to be. I tried to operate on the premise that the chief should be relieved of all the burdens of routine, that if necessary I would make a mistake in signing a paper rather than bother him unnecessarily with something that he didn't really have to be concerned with. He had plenty of problems of his own, as I found out later on, at the higher levels of the

Washington political-military scene, notably the relationships with Congress. These were the chief's and unless he was ill or incapacitated, should never be anybody else's. Notably, the relationships with the Appropriation Committees of the House and the Senate in defense of the budget. Really, throughout my time and his time also, you were never very far from this concern about the budget. First, getting the money appropriated, then getting it approved through the Bureau of the Budget, since unfortunately, and I think devilishly, the Bureau of the Budget now assists you in spending the money as well as telling you what you can ask Congress for in the first place. I'll come back to this later on when I talk about the business of being chief.

Q: Just one observation, one question, about that. In that time, the appropriations for a fiscal year were made in advance of a fiscal year. That's not the case now.

Adm. W.: There was already beginning to be a lag then, as early as 1956, ~~1956, 1957~~, but nothing like the catastrophic lag that now exists of upwards of a year between the time your last appropriation lapses and your next appropriation is really made.

Q: Is that a stultifying thing?

Adm. W.: Oh, yes, because you're confined to spending at a no higher level than you did last year in all the departments. How they find it possible to operate at all is beyond my comprehension. I don't know. I think it's only done by informal contact between the military and the responsible committee members in the House and the Senate. They have to give their concurrence to what must be done in order to operate.

Q: Is this a justifiable development in the system?

Adm. W.: The system, right or wrong, has grown up through the years. You first must authorize an appropriation, then put up the money, and this is done by separate committees. How this happened or why in the dim days of the first Congress after the Constitution was adopted, I have no idea. I've always been intereste[d] in this question. You have to have twice as many committees, obviously. The Armed Services Committee authorizes, and the Appropriations Committee of the Armed Services Sub-committee appropria[tes] and both of these cows are exceedingly sacred on the Hill, and I'[m] sure the system is never going to get changed.

Q: Is it an extension of checks and balances?

Adm. W.: Presumably. I don't know, but it's the way the power is divided in the Congress, and this is so thoroughly embedded in tradition and in the pride of individual congressmen and senators that I'm sure it will never get changed. It's a long process. Wh[y] the lag gets worse and worse, I don't understand, but I'm afraid that the only reasonable supposition is that the Congress is just not efficient and getting less so. The method that was adequate one hundred years ago is not good any more. It's not fast enough.

We were speaking of my relief of Rear Admiral Parsons as depu[ty] chief of the Bureau of Ordnance. This naval officer-scientist was a man of strong personal beliefs and convictions and great strengt[h] of character. He insisted in spite of all obstacles in supporting at the Naval Ordnance Test Center at China Lake, then called Inyok[ern] the development of a Sidewinder missile - air-to-air missile - eve[n] though there was no money available for this purpose. Somehow or other, he diverted the necessary amount of money from other appropriations to keep the project alive.

Q: What was his vision in this matter?

Adm. W.: As a non-aviator, I simply can't tell you. I think his vision was simply his belief in the integrity and technical ability of Dr. McLean, who invented it and who against all odds pushed the project through to completion. The heart of the missile is in the infrared sensor in the nose. There were something like forty different models attempted experimentally before any missile showed any sign of having seen the target at all. But McLean refused to quit, he refused to believe that his concept was scientifically wrong. It was right, and eventually he evolved a solution. Here was a lethal air-to-air missile which was obtainable in quantity production for something less than five thousand dollars a round and has been proven since in war, in action, and it wouldn't have been in the arsenal of the United States - it was used probably more by the Air Force than the Navy in the end - had it not been for the vision of Admiral Parsons in supporting the project. I believe that the higher authorities, who were even then beginning to proliferate in the Pentagon, repeatedly told him that this project was no good - cancel it, and he refused.

It is not possible in the bureaucracy, as it has grown like the algae in a polluted lake like Erie, to do anything like this any more. I'm not at all sure that there's room in the piled-up, layer upon layer, Navy Department and the Department of Defense and the Congress for any idea to live to fruition any more. Somebody will shoot it down.

Q: That's a pretty terrible indictment.

Adm. W.: That's right, but I'm afraid this is true.

Q: Is there not any attempt at the marriage of a scientific mind with a non-scientific one in administrative control?

Adm. W.: There's an enormous machine. You have to have an operational requirement. You have to have a whole bale of paper. Much of this was generated during the McNamara regime and it has not been changed significantly since. The same man who's carrying over, Foster, is head of research and development, who was there under the Johnson administration. If it doesn't fit into the machinery of the bureaucracy, it's no good, and I'm afraid for the future of the United States, frankly. I speak with the utmost seriousness. I don't think a good idea for something that's simpler, easier, or better, has a chance to survive in the present system of controls. But, on a happier note, the Sidewinder did and it was entirely due, in my opinion, to the strength of mind and the singleness of purpose of Admiral Parsons. All I had to do was aid and abet the skulduggery a little bit, because by the time he died and I took over from him and was Admiral Schoeffel's deputy, the project was well on the way to success.

Q: Well, Admiral, this was in the early to middle fifties, do you imply, then, that the climate has changed so totally in this...

Adm. W.: The climate has changed disastrously for the worse, in my opinion. There are so many layers and layers and layers upon layers

Q: Is this due to the proliferation in the Department of Defense itself?

Adm. W.: This is part of it. One part is the obsessive fear that somebody's going to waste a dollar, so they lose hundreds of millions of dollars instead on the C-5A or the newest Army tank or the F-14 Navy fighter or the Mark 48 torpedo - you name it. It's all the same, the same dreary story of failure. I'm afraid, frankly, for the United States.

Q: Where is the wisdom of the Congress in this picture, or is there any wisdom?

Adm. W.: There is a great deal of wisdom. Some of the most knowledgeable men, unfortunately, like Harry Shepherd from California and Wigglesworth of Massachusetts, are dead and gone. They knew where practically all the dead bodies were buried and they knew a phony from a real when an officer was on the stand, and they could literally almost flay a witness if they knew he was not speaking from his own knowledge and from his own belief. I know because I was there for three years, and I got my ulcer there! I loved both those old men.

Q: I've had a picture of Richard Wigglesworth and his inquisitive mind, knowing the answer to a question before he asked it.

Adm. W.: Yes. He was interested more than anybody in Washington in the Navy's ammunition and he knew a great deal more about this subject than I did to start with. In the first year I appeared, I ended up in a pool of sweat in the chair. There was nothing left of Withington but this pool. The next year I was much better prepared, and this was part of the genesis of my ulcer. I'm afraid that knowledgeable men like this are not being developed i[n] Congress as much as they were, and this is bad for the United Sta[tes].

Q: Is there a greater turnover today in the Congress?

Adm. W.: Maybe there's not as much personal specialization in the affairs of the military. I don't know. I couldn't tell you. It may be that there are congressmen and senators coming along an[d] following in the footsteps of people like Vinson and Shepherd and Wigglesworth. I don't know. I don't see much sign of it.

Q: This would tend to offset, would it not, if we did have, the developments in the Department of Defense?

Adm. W.: Yes, it would. I wish I could see some improvement in the inter-service war, but I don't. The strongest Secretary of Defense, I suppose, by general agreement, was McNamara, yet the war rages unabated, and it still does under his successor. And th[is] is a part of the roles and missions game. We were speaking earli[er] of the cognizance game in the Navy. Who had the power? Who will exercise it, and will he do it wisely or not? That last question appears to be the least important sometimes.

Well, to return to the assistant chief days. The Sidewinder missile program began to show results. The first missiles showed some interest in the drone targets at Inyokern and they hit them [and] destroyed them. This is a heat-seeking missile, as you know, and [when] it hits the target it goes right down the tailpipe of the engine [of] the airplane, and this is not very good for the airplane. They used to try at Inyokern to conserve on the drone targets by carry[ing] flares on the wing tips of the drones and the heat-seeker missile would, hopefully, home on the flare as a hotter source rather than the tailpipe of the jet engine, but there was a distressingly high loss rate in the drones. When the missile went into quantity production after I became chief, and was ordered by the Air Force as well as the Navy, then there was a question about the producer. This is one of the illegal procedures in which I participated as chief.

The Philco Corporation, before it was absorbed by Ford Motors, was the sole producer. They had worked out the initial production model with Inyokern. We very carefully worked in the General Electric Company as a second source.

Q: For competition?

Adm. W.: For competition and to keep the price down, certainly. And the first year the competitive bids came in, the General Electric bid was so much higher than the Philco bid for approximately the same number that we obviously couldn't accept it. So here we were stuck with a sole source of procurement, which is death for the government in any item. So, I got on the telephone and called a senior vice president of the General Electric Company - the man who was directly responsible for all military procurements, not the president. I don't remember his name, and wouldn't tell it to you if I could. I said, "I don't have a recorder on my end of the telephone, as I assume you don't have any either, because if you show me a transcript later, I'll deny it. But I want to tell you that I want to keep you in business as a competitor for Philco and with your present bid price I can't do it. Look at the figures and give me a new number," and hung up the telephone. Within, I guess, less than a week, I had a new quote and we had two sources of supply for the GC andA.

Q: That was a more compatible bid?

Adm. W.: Oh, yes. We could accept both bids. G C and A is what the bidders were bidding on and this is the heart of the missile. The nose of it, the infrared sensor, the controls, the wings, et cetera, not the rocket or the warhead.

Well, I'm still not quite through as assistant chief am I?

Q: No. Let me ask. This missile, was it entirely unique at that stage with us or was it a concept that the Russians understood or the British understood?

Adm. W.: The basis of the missile, as of many other missiles, was the solid-propellant rocket. The Bureau of Aeronautics concurrently was developing a liquid-fueled air-to-air missile. I don't remember what the name of it was. Theoretically then, and I think now, you can put more energy - propulsive energy - into a liquid-fueled rocket than you can into a solid-fueled rocket, and a great deal of solid evidence can be produced in support of both sides. I'll come to this later in more detail on the Polaris program.

Q: Was the Bureau of Ordnance cognizant of their developments in the liquid fuel area?

Adm. W.: This was another problem. This was an air-to-air missile and it presumably should have been produced in the Bureau of Aeronautics yet it was invented in the Bureau of Ordnance. This was probably the most difficult problem of all. However, eventually we were very proud because the Bureau of Aeronautics had to assign a Sidewinder Project officer in the Bureau of Aeronautics. They accepted the weapon.

Q: Tell me in some sense how this was developed, how it was achieved.

Adm. W.: Through an historical process which is not quite clear to me the enormous research and development station on the desert at China Lake was developed by the Bureau of Ordnance, primarily for rockets, and it turned out, most importantly, that they were air-to-air rockets rather than surface-to-air rockets for the Navy. The guiding spirit behind this program was a wonderful man from Denmark named Lauritsen, who was a professor at California Institute of Technology. He trudged out in the desert and found this place. "Inyokern" means that this enormous desert area is partly in Inyo and partly in Kern counties in central southern California, more or less in sight of Mount Whitney. Dr. Lauritsen was personally convinced that the rocket had a future in the military services. He was sort of the descendant of Dr. Goddard, and he is personally responsible for a great deal of the productive work in the desert under Caltech before the end of World War II and subsequent to World War II after Caltech, in fact, cut out of the rocket business, as such.

Q: How long after World War II were these scientists who were university-oriented interested in military things?

Adm. W.: This varied with the man, of course. Dr. Lauritsen

continued to be interested at NOTS - Naval Ordnance Test Station until his death as a member of the Board of Advisers. That is not quite the correct phrase, but that is what he was. I was a member of this board after I retired in 1961, and one of my most joyous memories is of being with him at these large board meeting We were all supposed to have a finite tenure of office, but there was always a good reason why Dr. Lauritsen shouldn't be relieved. In fact, I don't think he was ever relieved until he died. A man of great wisdom and great productivity for his adopted country.

Q: Is he the exception or were other scientists ...

Adm. W.: Other scientists were on the board, of course, but they varied, but Charlie Lauritsen was always there. Nobody ever woul agree that he should be relieved and nobody could conceive of any body competent to relieve him with equal background and interest and drive and intelligence.

In addition to the Sidewinder, which was really an upstart program stolen from the Bureau of Aeronautics by the Bureau of Ordnance, there was the program of ship-to-air missiles which wer developed by the Applied Physics Laboratory at Silver Spring. Th was an outfit, and I believe still is an outfit, supported by the Bureau of Ordnance and now by its successor, the same outfit under the name of Ordnance Systems Command. The laboratory is operated by the Johns Hopkins University.

Q: Did Dr. Tuve operate it?

Adm. W.: Yes. Dr. Tuve was really the founder of the laboratory. It was started and founded for scientific research and development in World War II to develop the VT fuse, the radio-controlled fuse for naval guns, and that development after our herculean efforts was a success, as you know.

The Applied Physics Laboratory has had a distinguished record in the field of science and in the field of engineering development. The family of missiles which has evolved from their efforts has included the Terrier, Talos, the Tartar, and something which is now called, I believe, the standard missile. These are only the missiles which reached the fleet. A number more have been experimented on and later canceled because of expense or other difficulties. The Triton program was one of them. Through the years, this outfit of scientists and engineers has been supported through the Bureau of Ordnance under contract. This concept of working for the government but not being in or of it has a good many advantages. There have been other laboratories like it. There is still one at Penn State University under the Bureau of Ordnance. There used to be one in Seattle supported by the University of Washington which has unfortunately recently gone by the board.

Q: Because of the student business?

Adm. W.: Because of the students. Primarily because of student nihilism, I guess that's a pretty good word. I'm surprised in view of the recent disturbances at Penn State that the underwater laboratory is still functioning there. There is a water tunnel and a corps of good scientists and a backbone of competent graduate students who do most of the work in all of these government-supported laboratories.

Q: Would you say that one of the virtues of this extension of the research is the fact that it's not under Civil Service?

Adm. W.: I'm afraid it's correct to say that there is a stultifying influence in the Civil Service. I hate to say this, having been the skipper of NOL, which, of course, is Civil Service and having been an adviser since retirement at a number of the government laboratories. I believe, by and large, that there is more - at least, the scientists think there's more - freedom to operate in a non-Civil-Service activity, rather than in one where they are part of the government bureaucracy.

Before I took over from Admiral Schoeffel as chief there was generating in the industry and through the Applied Physics Laboratory at Silver Spring under Johns Hopkins, a family of ship-to-air missiles. The principal contractors were the Convair people at Pomona in a large plant built by the government in southern California, and Bendix at South Bend, Indiana, on the Talos missile, which was a very large ram-jet, air-breathing missile. Once one of these sizable missile programs gets started, it has an inherent life of its own and all hell can't stop it. It may be promising, it may be a dog, it may be doubtful, but it's almost impossible to stop the missile program.

Q: Why, Sir?

Adm. W.: I can't quite tell you. There are always its zealous proponents in uniform, in the laboratories and in industry. They are always ready to tell you that success is just around the corner, if it's obviously a failure or if it's marginal. They're always ready to tell you that so much money's been invested that you have to invest more and then we're going to get the pay-off. These are just some of the arguments in favor.

Q: It's a one-way road, then?

Adm. W.: Yes. Very seldom do you find a congressman with the strength of mind that Mr. Hebert showed the other day in withholding eight hundred million dollars from the F-15 fighter because the Navy couldn't explain the cost. This very seldom happens in the Congress. It should happen oftener. It should have happened with the Mark 48 torpedo. It should have happened with the C-5A aircraft, and so forth and so on. There is no excuse for these enormous wastages of government money. The Navy has to have a reasonably good case for this new fighter or it's not going to be built, and I think Mr. Hebert is entirely correct.

Well, we were speaking about the longevity of the missile programs. I can understand the reluctance in the Department of Defense research and development empire to approve any new program, because they look back over their shoulders at the inherent longevity of all of these missile programs and other programs that nobody seems ever able to stop.

Q: When did the first of the missile programs begin?

Adm. W.: I suppose possibly with Regulus I in the Bureau of Aeronautics a long time ago, which, of course, was a small drone airplane with primitive guidance in it, and a pretty good weapon. The much improved supersonic Regulus II never really got off the ground, so to speak. I think only one actual shot was ever fired. Yet if we'd pursued these weapons, we would have been far ahead of the present Russian version of ship-to-ship missiles, the Styx missile system which they fire from Komar gunboats, of which they have hundreds and of which we have none.

Well, by the time I relieved Admiral Schoeffel, we were well along in the ship-to-air missile program, the air-to-air program, Sidewinder, was showing great promise of being successful, the whole ordnance picture of the postwar Navy looked reasonably good. There was an understandable, almost complete, hiatus in the Navy building program since we ended World War II with such an enormous armada of ships. The question mostly was what should we keep rather than what should we build. And while there was a great deal of thought about the future, there wasn't very much money being invested in it in the way of new ship construction or indeed new airplanes, either.

Q: Was there harmony within the Navy on objectives and determinations? For instance, were the submarine boys in harmony with the..

Adm. W.: I think, in general, my impression from the material bureau point of view was that there was harmony among the planners on the Pentagon side, yes, in the office of the Chief of Naval Operations. Of course, there were homeric arguments about whether we should spend more money on mines or on torpedoes or on submarines or on destroyers or on airplanes or on aircraft carriers, and so on. But these were all healthy. They're bound to happen always. They should happen. If you have a good case, you win. If you don't have a good case, you lose. And if you have a fair case, you'll compromise.

Things were not particularly urgent-looking on the international horizon or on the technical horizon or on the interservice wars horizon when I took over the Bureau of Ordnance in 1955. The first event which ruffled the surface, and really significantly ruffled the surface, was the advent of the Polaris program, which didn't start out under that name at all. There is a very splendid account of the early days of the program in the Naval Review annual of 1970, a year ago May. I read it just recently. This is written by a retired captain who obviously was there when the battles were fought, and from my own knowledge of the Bureau of Ordnance, it is substantially correct in all details.

I don't know who first thought of the idea of the seaborne delivery of strategic missiles against Russian targets. I don't know who was the author. There were probably many authors. There was great discussion after the idea was generated, and I think before even the first sacred requirements paper was written upon which a development must be based now in the system of bureaucracy. At any rate, the idea was that we should bombard the Russian heartland and presumably kill as many people as possible in the process from the sea, shooting, preferably submerged, from submarines. The firing ships would be an invulnerable target up until the time it was decided that the button had been pressed, we must go to war, and shoot before the Russians shot first. This argument obviously will continue ad infinitum as obviously both scorpions are in the bottle.

The thought of firing a missile from a submerged submarine raised a whole host of problems: How do you do this? Speaking very crudely, Firestone and Henry Ford and Thomas Edison were great friends in the old days, and one of them said - it's no longer important which one - "Why don't we have internal combustion engines in submarines and just use these engines submerged? Henry

Ford replied, "Have you ever farted in a bathtub?" This is one of the most a'propos comments I've ever heard about a technical subject. A very similar business of technical restrictions applies to shooting anything submerged. You have an enormous bubble of energy going out into the water from your launching tubes. What do you do about it?

Q: With some restraints!

Adm. W.: Yes. There were many technical questions about how you would build a submarine with all these holes in it - 16 holes, presumably, for sixteen missile-firing tubes. You'd have to have these holes sealed when the ship was submerged, obviously.

Q: Were 16 anticipated at the beginning?

Adm. W.: I don't know how many. It doesn't matter. The whole concept was the same no matter whether it was 2, 4, or 8, 16 or 5. Obviously, you'd have to have a big ship, a bigger ship than we'd ever conceived of as a submersible with nuclear power. Everybody agreed from the start that it would have to have nuclear power, and since we knew how to make a reactor system from earlier successful submarines, it was obvious that the Rickover group would have to design the power plant. This was obvious from the start.

Q: You imply that the idea originated in that group, then?

Adm. W.: Oh, no, I couldn't say.

There were obviously several claimants to be the prime developer in this Polaris picture. The major one, I presume, was the Bureau of Ordnance, naturally. Another one was the Bureau of

Aeronautics because they had more experience with big missiles. They had had Regulus-1 and Regulus-2. They had a very good case.

Well, it was pretty clear - Arleigh Burke was CNO at about this time - that unless this program, this idea, had top-level backing and top-level priority and a lot of money, it would never get anywhere. I think with great wisdom - I believe Arleigh himself made the decision - of course, he recommended it to the Secretary and the Secretary announced the decision - it was decided that there would be a Secretary's committee responsible for this development, that there would be a single developmental czar, and the czar would be responsible to the Secretary, through the committee, and to nobody else. And the Bureaus then in existence, most importantly Aeronautics and Ordnance, would be bypassed except as supporting activities.

Q: Was this wisdom derived from some other experience?

Adm. W.: No. I think it more or less came out of the blue. Here was a project which had very active opposition by many people and it was obviously going to absorb a lot of money which other Navy claimants could very well use - carrier construction, airplane construction, destroyer construction, mine construction, you name it.

Q: Yes, but we were in a new age and wasn't it obvious?

Adm. W.: It wasn't at all obvious that the Navy should do this. The Air Force said, oh, we will do it all, and they still say it, if you ask them. The Army was then - and this is one of the most interesting parts of the exercise early in the game - developing what was called a Jupiter missile, which was a liquid-fueled missile, and initially the Navy went into partnership with the Army hoping that one missile would do for their purposes and for ours too in the submarine. Before Raborn was even ordered to Washington, I with Admiral Sides negotiated with the Army on this missile. This was during the time when Admiral Sides was the missile czar in CNO. Everybody was afraid of liquid propellants under water, and I think that if one of these things ever caused a fire the ship was lost, and if you had a thermonuclear explosion along with the fire you'd have had a real mess on your hands. Everybody felt that if solid-propellant rockets could be developed with the necessary capacity and impulse, it would be a damned sight safer to live with in a ship than a liquid-fueled rocket. I felt then, and I feel now, that this was the right answer, if this solid rocket could be developed.

Q: Was there a concommitant thought that we should have more widespread defense on water and land?

Adm. W.: It was the initial hope that the same rocket, liquid-fueled rocket, the Jupiter missile, could serve the needs of both Army and Navy. Whether this weapon would have been fired by the Air Force or the Army is irrelevant. It was a system which, hopefully, could work on land and at sea.

Q: What I meant is was it the current thought that land-based missiles were not really sufficient in the face of the enemy and it was necessary to spread out to the sea as well? Was that a part of the thinking in those days?

Adm. W.: Yes, it was a part of the thinking from the start that a fixed launching point was inherently inferior to a movable launching pad, especially, hopefully, a movable launching point which could not be located, that is to say, from a submarine.

Well, the negotiations with the Army were difficult, but not unfriendly. They were, I should say, conducted at a very high level in the Pentagon. And as we began to understand that a large liquid rocket was feasible, not too much internecine war occurred when the Navy said we would prefer to go the solid rocket way for a submersible missile project rather than the Jupiter. Jupiter did turn out to be a success and was one of the earlier of the Army family of missiles. About the time that we won this war with the Army, if you could call it a war, Raborn was selected by Admiral Burke to be the head of the project, and he came to Washington and started stealing my best people and the best people from the Bureau of Aeronautics, the Bureau of Supplies and Accounts, and everybody else in Washington and anywhere else he could find.

Q: What had been his reputation that caused him to be called?

Adm. W.: He was a very fine naval aviator with a good reputation in the field of weapons. Where he got it, I don't know, because he was not a postgraduate officer. He was known to have drive, intelligence, and capacity for carrying responsibility, all of which he showed to the greatest advantage in the successful Polaris project.

It was obvious that the only way to handle this business from my point of view and from the Aeronautics' point of view, was to give him unstinted support, otherwise he had no chance to succeed.

Withington # 2 - 1

I mean real support, not just words, so that when he came and said he had to have so and so to work for him full time, I stuttered and stammered and hollered, but I let him go. I felt I had to. I knew that if I didn't do it, he'd go to the Secretary and the Secretary would order me to let him go.

Q: Had you had any words with Arleigh Burke on this subject? Was he backing him to the hilt also?

Adm. W.: Yes.

Q: Well, did he request you to do so?

Adm. W.: He didn't have to. He told Raborn - this is in this Institute article a year ago, May - if there's any real indication that you aren't going to make this project go, you come to me immediately and I'll cancel it. Of course, he never had to do that. The first thing Raborn did after he started to gather this star-studded organization - and I mean it was star-studded, it was probably the most effective technical organization that Washington has ever seen - the first thing he did himself was to head a survey team to pick a prime contractor for the missile project, and he spent some months at this, the first two or three months really of the project itself.

Q: Was he bound by the usual government rules that you had to have competitive bidders and that kind of thing?

Adm. W.: No, not really. He asked for proposals from several different current prime contractors. He evaluated these proposals, visited the prospective contractors, and talked to the people who would work on the project, if successful. Then he came to me and

Withington # 2 - 157

"Lockheed is it, now what'll I do?" I said, "Red, if you want to be the head man in this project really, you announce this selection to the press, and then tell the Secretary what you've done." And that is exactly what he did do. It's exactly what would be totally impossible in present-day bureaucratic Washington. But, in my opinion, it was exactly the success of the project. He was the boss and everybody knew it.

Q: How did the Secretary react to this?

Adm. W.: He swallowed many, many times, I think, but he never came back at Red or at me.

Q: Who was he? Tom Gates?

Adm. W.: No, I forget now. It was before Gates. Maybe it was. By that time I knew Mr. Gates very well, and he knew me, and I'm sure that he had just as much confidence in me as I had in him. I feel sure he knew that I had good reasons for advising Red to do what I did. I said to Red, "Now, if this comes back to you and you get bitten by the Secretary, please refer everything to me. I'm responsible. I'm the adviser here." Well, I would do the same thing tomorrow in the same situation.

Q: Was there any repercussion from Congress at that point?

Adm. W.: No, not a peep.

Q: Had they been advised?

Adm. W.: No. This is another thing. He'd have to tell the local congressman what's going to happen. This is the local ground rule now and has been for a long time.

I think that Red had enough good sense himself to notify the interested California people on the QT that it was going to be Lockheed. Maybe, I did. I don't remember now. This is a little hazy. We both knew that this was important, anyway!

The project continued to eat up a good many of my best people. For a long time he didn't have any contract section of his own, and my contract people did all his work, and everything was on a "must be completed yesterday" basis. That's indeed the only way he could run the project and make it go on time schedule, which eventually he met.

Q: Who established a time schedule for him?

Adm. W.: The Secretary did on his recommendation, and he beat it in the end. I believe he met or exceeded every target date that he set. It is the great success story of the postwar Navy, in my opinion, technically.

Q: And this involved the proliferation of industry?

Adm. W.: Oh, I don't know how many people are in the family now - the Polaris family - at least 50 are important in this project. He used to call in people on Saturday morning from all over the country, routinely, during the height of the program, and work, a work, and work on the weak spots. And he'd call the head people of the companies to account if things weren't going well.

Q: This sounds somewhat comparable to World War II enterprises.

Adm. W.: It was more or less carried out on the basis of the Manhattan Project, in a smaller way, but of course much smaller in amount of money, although very significant amounts of money. This is why there was so much opposition within the Navy because we all knew it was absorbing lots of Navy money which could have been used elsewhere, and a great deal of the best talent the Navy had.

Q: How secret was it kept? What were the regulations covering that?

Adm. W.: It was not on a Manhattan Project at all. The newspapers were pretty well kept aware of what was going on. They knew what the project was, the reasons for it, and generally speaking whether the progress was good, bad, or indifferent. And, indeed, it was outstandingly good from the start.

Q: We weren't at all concerned about the potential enemy knowing?

Adm. W.: No, I don't think we ever felt that.

Q: Did we know whether they were engaged in a similar project?

Adm. W.: I was not aware of such knowledge if we had it at the time. We knew that sooner or later they would be. This was obvious because the idea of the invulnerable launching point is so attractive.

Q: But not so pressing with the Russians as with us because their land mass is so much greater.

Adm. W.: Yes, but they're a long way except for shooting over the pole, from getting at us through the air. As you probably know, their initial efforts involved firing missiles from the surface.

They have only a few today as far as I know, of missile-firing submarines that can launch submerged.

This article in the Naval Institute a year ago May attacks the question of why 41 Polaris submarines. This has always puzzle[d] me, too. Apparently it generated from a series of rather off-the-cuff remarks by Arleigh Burke. He was thinking out loud, and eventually these thoughts got congelaed into a program and got into a funding-cycle.

It's a little inaccurate to say that my time as chief was entirely devoted to supporting Raborn and the Polaris project, although this was probably the most important single activity we had. We didn't realize it at the time. We had to keep the Navy going. We had to testify before the Ships Characteristics Board. This is the committee which has for years been designing naval ships and, I think, generally doing a very poor job of it. The genesis of a Navy ship has always been a fearful and wonderful story. For year[s] when I was young there was something in Washington called the General Board. This was composed of the senior admirals of the Na[vy] who were on their last cruise before retiring. They presumably ha[d] a good deal of wisdom to offer, and indeed they did, and they were the ones who considered proposals for new Navy ships and weapons. They no longer exist. The function of generating ship design now given to the Ships Characteristics Board, and this is a large committee with representation from the Chief of Naval Operations and office and the material bureaus of the Navy, now called the Materi[al] Commands under the Chief of Naval Material. Like all committees, the consensus very often is not the best solution. Everybody want[s] to cram into this ship the maximum protection, the maximum speed, the maximum armor, the maximum of electronic capability - you name it. If we have it, or even have heard of it in the newspaper or some technical journal we want it. The result often is a ship that is a bad compromise, which is crammed with machinery and electronic equipment, and which has inadequate facilities for the comfort and health of the officers and men who man it. I'm afraid it's true that in spite of air-conditioning and other modern inventions, the modern ship is not anywhere near as comfortable, man per man, as the USS Constitution possibly was, thinking about the cubic capacity of the berthing spaces versus the number of men in the crew.

Q: Does this group also deal with new types of ships?

Adm. W.: Yes. They're the ones who approve the characteristics of a proposed new ship, and this is a very difficult, involved, and complex procedure involving many meetings and much shuffling of hugh piles of paper.

Q: Would they not, Sir, as a presumably younger group and more au courant to the situation, would they not do a better job in the areas of new types nowadays than the General Board could have done?

Adm. W.: This is very likely so, yes. I don't know. This is a matter, of course, of opinion. But you still have a question of designing by committee and this has some disadvantages as well as the advantage of hearing all the different points of view.

Q: But then the actual design work has to get down to the naval architect, doesn't it?

Adm. W.: Of course, and this is, I suppose - I know, as a matter of fact - the most difficult problem in modern building of a ship. The so-called interfaces between the systems - aeronautics, ships, ordnance, supply, medical, all of the activities of the Navy have responsibilities toward this ship and they meet in the ship, and the most difficult interface I can think of at the moment is the fire control switchboard, where the heart of the gunnery system and the missile system goes through the switchboard and meets the power supply which is provided by the Bureau of Ships. And if all of the connections don't mesh nothing works. It's just as simple as that. So there are whole companies - the Vitro Company in Silver Spring is one of them - who get their livelihood from trying to solve all of the interface problems before it's too late. That is to say, before the ship is built and the mistake is embedded in iron, steel, wires, and pipes.

Q: The whole question of fire control in ships has changed greatly from World War II, has it not?

Adm. W.: Yes, the complexity is - oh, perhaps not a factor of ten greater, but it's very much greater.

Q: Would you talk about that area because it is one of some concern

Adm. W.: The first fire control computer was the Mark I Rangekeeper which was invented by a genius named Hannibal Ford, who also invented the signal system of the New York subway. It was a small instrument - circular instrument - maybe 12 inches deep, on a tripod, with one handle with which you wound the spring motor, and an integrator which ground out the range depending upon the range rate you had set upon it, and there were components for our ships and target motion and the estimated range. Later, he added a little appendage which gave you some idea of what the deflection effects of the wind might be. But this was all there was to it. There was nothing electrical, nothing complicated, there was nothing that could break, really, except the main spring in the motor that ran the disc which was the integrator. There was a ball on the integrator which was positioned in accordance with the relative posiion of your own ship and the target, and their speeds and courses.

From this Mark L Rangekeeper developed much more elaborate, but still mechanical computer type. We went into World War II with a modern version of the mechanical computer, both for main battery and for anti-aircraft batteries in use, and those computers worked magnificently. Even by that time the electrical complexity of the switchboard in the plotting room was very considerable, and here was the major interface between ordnance and ships, since the Bureau of Ships provided all those switches, and the inputs and outputs through the switchboard came from the Brueau of Ordnance applied instruments, the instruments, the plotting room, the local instruments at the guns and the turrets and gun mounts of the ship.

Now we have electronic computers and so-called digital computers. The NTDS, the Naval Tactical Data System, is supplied by the Bureau of Ships. We're submerged in a sea of vacuum tubes and their successors which are, as you know, much smaller. They're little chips of matter which perform the same function that the vacuum tubes do, which the British call valves. In the process of this electrification and electronification of the Navy, we have reduced greatly the size of our computers. We have, I'm afraid, also increased significantly our reliability problem, our maintenance problem, and I know we've significantly increased our cost. Why this should be is not quite clear to me. The repetitive nature of these little marvelous electrical and electronic devices is just wonderful, and it certainly ought to be cheaper to make one of the electronic chips by the hundreds than it should be to make an electric-hydraulic mechanical computer, with its integrators, its differentials – mechanical differentials – and all the rest of the things that the Ford Instrument Company used to make so well.

Among other things, the mechanical computer invariably involve errors throughout because of the slack, the lost motion between gears and shafts and so on. There is no electrical or electronic lost motion because the atoms move at the speed of light, which is 186,000 miles a second. So there is this inherent superiority of the electronic computer. But you have to find somebody who can maintain the equipment. As far as the operation is concerned it's probably very little different in complexity, as far as training concerned, the training of operators. He doesn't have to know what causes the dial to move in order to do what the dial tells him to

This reminds me of an old story of World War I. The British were the first to develop any sort of centralized fire control in their major ships, and one of my predecessors in the Ordnance gam went as an observer to the Grand Fleet. When the general alarm b rang, he went down to the plotting room to observe what happened. A lot of great big Cockney-type marines came down, and each man l up in the plotting room facing the wall. He had a dial in front him with a bug that went around one ring and he, with a crank, powered the motion from that bug to the other. And that was the step-by-step transmission system, and that's what made the fire control system work. And he said presently all you could smell in that plotting room was feet!

This, in an exaggerated fashion, is the story of the old-fashioned mechanical computer versus the modern devices. They brought their advantages. They brought their disadvantages.

Q: Some of this developed under your aegis, did it not?

Adm. W.: Yes. I was a little bit uncertain. One thing I did state when I took over from Admiral Schoeffel, although I had the title of chief, I guaranteed to everybody in the Bureau and out of it, including the contractors, that I would never personally try to invent anything, and I never did. I just tried to look with a jaundiced eye and ask embarrassing questions of all the inventors who came into the office. This, I figured then, and am still convinced of now, is the correct attitude for the chief to assume.

Q: Did this particular chief have aptitude in invention?

Adm. W.: No, neither then, earlier, nor later.. The best grasp the chief ever got, and I'm sure this is still true, of what was going on was the annual review of the activities of the Bureau involved in the presentation and preparation of the budget for Congress. I would spend the better part of two weeks with my senior people tearing the budget request to pieces, trying to put myself on the other side of the table on Capitol Hill in the committee hearing room, trying to imagine what the most embarrassing question might be that the congressmen could ask of me, which I would find it most difficult to answer. And this was the most interesting exercise I really ever had as chief. I reduced some of my people I don't know whether to ulcers or not, but to tears because they couldn't answer my questions, and I would just adjourn the meeting and tell them to come back when they could!

Q: You were going to be on the...

Adm. W.: Certainly. I had to answer all these questions. Of course, sometimes I was caught very short and that's what gave me my ulcer, I guess. Nobody is ever perfect, and I was never able entirely to anticipate what the questions might be. Mr. Wigglesworth was just wonderful with questions concerning the ammunition supply of the Navy. But this annual review was, as I say, the time of year when the chief really had to find out what was going on, had to understand it.

Mr. Forrestal, when he was Secretary, used to come to our monthly R and D meetings, and he would sit there and listen with great interest and every once in a while he'd put in his oar. One day a kid from the research department was talking about a problem about adhesives. Oh, heavens, I think he was trying to develop a nose covering for a use that would stand up in storage, and Mr. Forrestal looked over his glasses at him and said, "Son, did you ever try glue?"!

Q: Did hydrographics make any contribution in the R and D area?

Adm. W.: No. We had occasional meaningful cooperation with the Office of Naval Research. Their field, of course, was and is basic research and not developing weapons, but one of their scientists appeared unannounced at my door one day and told me of a superb idea he had to sniff the launching of rockets. I don't remember any details. I shouldn't probably speak of them if I did. This man had authority from his chief of Naval Research to come and see me, and I immediately gave him some money because I recognized at once that the project had great promise and I think it paid off later. This was unusual that there'd be this direct communication between anybody working for the Office of Naval Research and the active people in the field of weapons. That's why I remember it so clearly.

It was very heart-warming to me afterwards. This man had come to me with the assurance he'd get a reasonable hearing, an open-minded hearing. I guess this is one of the great satisfactions I had in the Navy because I had developed such a real rapport with the scientific and engineering men.

Q: Did this spring in part from your service on the <u>Mississippi</u>?

Adm. W.: I got it basically at NOL when I had to operate what was essentially a civilian establishment and persuade the senior ones that it was worthwhile, postwar, to remain as government servants instead of returning to universities and to industry.

Q: Admiral, in this period, this time at the beginning of the period, we witnessed almost a torrent of new types of vessels, naval vessels, coming into being. Did they constitute the chicken or the egg in terms of ordnance? Did ordnance developments precede the development of new types of ships, or was it the other way around?

Adm. W.: It almost has to be the other way around because the ship isn't going to wait. You have a contract with a shipbuilder for a certain hull, certain machinery, a certain delivery time schedule, and if you don't meet this with the ordnance equipment, you run into a delay pattern with additional cost to the Navy and additional payments to the shipbuilder. So you can't bet on, let's say, a new missile system and build your ship around it. You have to know before you order the ship that you have some sys that could be installed in it, and by such and such a date. And this is a very difficult problem indeed, and it's by no means always met successfully. But you cannot build blueprints into the ships. You have to have equipment to install in ships. This problem is always going to be with us.

There is a new ship-to-air and ship-to-ship missile system now under contract for the Navy, but I'm sure they have to be ver conservative about what ships they are going to guarantee it to b ready for installation in. I know they do from past experience. Everybody knows this.

Q: This great upsurge in new developments in terms of ships and of ordnance, is it based largely in the post World War II world o atomic energy, or are there other reasons for it? Were there oth lessons learned from the war that serve as a cause for all this?

Adm. W.: I'm thinking now also of what I've been hearing since retirement on my various advisory board assignments. The general trend in the development of airplanes is toward more speed and mo speed and more speed. You have to give away something, so that y give away either radius or ability to carry armament, or somethin

Then, a similar effort in missiles to get more range without throwing away too much payload in the process. This is inherently the Poseidon, the follow-on to Polaris. There is the effort to get a rocket assist projectile, or otherwise increase the range of a gun of a certain caliber without losing too much payload in the warhead, the HE charge in the projectile itself. There have been efforts to increase the efficiency of fusing, which is a very difficult subject in itself.

Everything we try to do involes more complexity and more cost, and I'm afraid we never learn and never will learn the lesson that you can't solve all your technical problems, your intractable problems of physics, simply by words you write in a specification, and if the contractor undertakes to manufacture a weapon or weapons system in accordance with your specifications and they're not feasible, he'll still sign a contract but it's your affair to get that system. You're either going to get no system or you're going to have to give him a series of waivers which water down the capability of the system which you have created initially on paper. There is the current problem [exaggeration] also of the contractors being hungry and buying into a program by underbidding other contractors with the hopeful intent that when he gets into trouble the government will bail him out. The Lockheed system is the current worst example.

Q: And supplemental appropriations.

Adm. W.: Oh yes.

Q: Admiral James was telling me the other day about a system which he helped to inaugurate with the deputy chief of the Department of

Defense wherein they were anticipating the total cost of something and that was it.

Adm. W.: This was tried under McNamara, but it was a dismal failure. They tried to do this with the C-5A, for instance. They tried it with the F-111, and look what happened.

Another thing which they hoped was their attempt to do research and development on a fixed-price-contract basis. This was attempted by Westinghouse with the Mark 48 torpedo, and the corporation lost something like fifty million dollars. They're still losing money as far as I know.

One of the great problems which will never be solved, I'm afraid, is the problem that the military is voracious and greedy and it always overwrites its specifications. This runs up the cost it runs up the time, and it's where the Russians are far smarter than we.

Q: How do you analyze this thinking on the part of the military?

Adm. W.: It's an impossible search toward perfection, I think.

Q: Is there the element of get it now while we can?

Adm. W.: I don't think so - perfectionism. It's hurt us badly for years, and it will always hurt us, I'm afraid.

Q: You don't always associate that perfectionism, idealism, with the military, however.

Adm. W.: This is the reason that Raborn succeeded so well in Polaris. They went for the attainable in every feature, and they got it. They put it on a time schedule and everything came out even.

Withington #3 - 172

Interview No. 3 with Rear Admiral Frederic F. Withington, U.S. Navy
(Retired)

Place: His home in Washington, D.C.

Date: Wednesday morning, 30 June 1971

Subject: Biography

By: John T. Mason, Jr.

Q: It's mighty nice to see you this morning, Sir.

Adm. W.: Glad you're with me.

Q: Last time you talked in some detail about your period of service as head of the Bureau of Ordnance. However, I think you want to add a few items to that chapter today, perhaps talking about the Bureau of Ordnance and budgetary matters.

Adm. W.: Yes. Toward the end of my three years plus as chief of the Bureau of Ordnance, the control by representatives of the Bureau of the Budget inside the Bureau of Ordnance and other Navy activities became more and more onerous. Generation of the budget is, of course, one of the fundamentally important functions the government has to carry out, and if there were not the Bureau of the Budget we would have to invent one. In addition to the difficulties involved in generating the budget, a system was allowed to develop where these same representatives of the Budget Bureau inside the government activities would have to approve expenditures after the money was appropriated. This extension of their power, in my opinion, was and still is a usurpation of the authority of the Secretary of Defense. I don't know whether the system is currently in operation in that way or not. I do know that all of the military operating activities are more circumscribed in what they can do and what authority is delegated to them than they were in my day, and in my day I felt specifically that this interference by the Bureau of the Budget was excessive and unwarranted.

Q: Well, Admiral, is this not an extension of the policy of the Congress as a whole, wherein they authorize certain projects but then there must be an appropriation after that to implement the authorization?

Adm. W.: The authorization and appropriation on Capitol Hill is one thing. The Bureau of the Budget is only concerned with appropriations. It has no concern at all with authorizations.

Toward the end of my tour as chief, I went to Detroit to make a speech and in a weak moment consented to a press interview. I didn't know at that time that it was wise always to tape record a press interview, so I did not do so. In the course of the interview, I made the remark that the Chief of the Bureau of Ordnance was a clerk in the Bureau of the Budget, referring to these budget analysts who were then infesting my activity. This hit the newspapers, and as soon as I got back to Washington I had to report to Mr. Franke, the under secretary of the Navy, who asked me (1) had I said this, (2) why had I said it, and didn't I think I'd done the Navy harm by saying it.

I had blurted out what I thought was the truth, and I had done so hopefully in the interests of the Navy. The director of the budget was understandably annoyed by this statement of mine, since the professional level of these men representing him was a lot higher than that of simply a clerk. By the publicity in connection with this incident I got a reputation for being quite tart of tongue and frank and open, so that when I was presented by the American Ordnance Association with the General Levin Campbell Gold Medal, there was a very large representation of all of the armament manufacturers then active in Washington, and I made a speech - I have it here in the form of a newspaper clipping by John G. Norris, who used to be the excellent reporter for The Washington Post. Perhaps it would be helpful if I simply read it into the record here

Q: I think you should, yes. And give me the date of it, please.

Adm. W.: I don't have the date, but it's 1958 - approximately February 1958. The article is headed Navy Ordnance Chief Hits Arms Cost Rise:

> In an unusually frank valedictory address the Navy's ordnance chief criticized himself and other arms officials yesterday for rapidly rising weapons costs. He offered a five-point plan to halt the trend. Rear Admiral F. S. Withington, Chief of the Navy Bureau of Ordnance, had this and some other pointed things to say at the American Ordnance Association's luncheon honoring him for his inspiring leadership in the timely arming of our fleet with the new weapons of the atomic age. He leaves next month to become commander of the United States Naval Forces in Japan. Rear Admiral Paul D. Stroop has been nominated as his successor. The AOA awarded Withington with General Levin H. Campbell's Gold Medal at a luncheon ceremony at the Mayflower Hotel.

Responding to the award, Withington summed up the Navy's future and present weapons situation. He said the major successful Navy developments during the past few years were the atomic depth charge, Betty, the guided missiles Sidewinder and Terrier, better torpedoes and mines, and the Talos missile-defense unit at White Sands.

Withington declared he didn't list the Talos itself as a missile accomplishment because in spite of some successful tests it did not get operational. It never did get operational. It was controlled from a shore station. There's been too much gap and not enough missiles in bragging about weapons recently, he added. The ordnance chief said that because of the long time it takes to develop arms, credit for the new weapons must go to his predecessors and that the success or failure of his own work must await appraisal of still-secret weapons not yet in service. This is because of the long lead time in all weapons development programs. But he admitted to one failure - an inability to keep weapons costs from rising. Instead of blaming this on inflation and greater complexity of weapons, Withington told his audience that some 500 arms manufacturers and military men must cut costs by (1) ingenuity and sound thinking in the initial engineering concept of new weapons; (2) more realistic specifications; (3) cost-conscious engineering; (4) use of standard stock components wherever possible; and (5) reducing the number of missiles programs, at least at the hardware stage.

That is the end of the quotation from my talk.

Q: Now, may I ask, was this speech taped?

Adm. W.: I think it was.

Q: You learned quickly!

Adm. W.: Yes. ~~This study, so to sp~~eak.

Q: Did you have any other brushes with the press during your regime?

Adm. W.: No, not in the Bureau of Ordnance. I had particularly good relationships with Mr. Norris who was then the military reporter for The Washington Post. Just as I was leaving, I again had to give a press interview, this time also taped, and had to announce regretfully that, at that time, the future of the Naval Gun Factory was very much in doubt. In fact, within a year after that it had to close because of competing prices with industry.

Q: You say it could not compete?

Adm. W.: Pricewise, yes, and this was sad because through the years a great deal of expertise had been developed there in guns, gunmounts, torpedo tubes, gun directors, and it had a very high quality optical shop.

Q: What was the underlying reason for its inability to compete any longer?

Adm. W.: One of the reasons was that all of the federal activities in town, notably headed by the White House, asked for work for nothing from the place and got it. This raised the overhead rates to an astounding number, and we just somehow never seemed to be able to drop this racket. So there we were.

Q: Yes, but I would think that in consideration of the whole project these free enterprises would have been added in.

Adm. W.: In government functions we had a very fine budget man who later left us in the Bureau of Ordnance and went with Raborn in the Polaris project. He kept track of our money much better than we had been able to do in previous regimes under naval officers - budget officers, so we knew where the money was going. The problem of how to stop the bleeding and leakage reflected in the overhead accounts from all the so-called cumshaw jobs that the gun factory did for everybody was seen to be beyond our solution. At least, my attempts were not successful.

Q: Admiral, what was the over-all budget of the Bureau of Ordnance?

Adm. W.: I can't remember any specific number.

Q: Roughly—

Adm. W.: It was rather large, on the order of hundreds of millions of dollars, and this is really an astonishing number when you consider that when I was a young officer in the 1930s, the Navy Department budget was less than 500 million dollars, the whole Navy Department.

Q: I suppose the word to describe all of that is "sophistication."

Adm. W.: Well, I don't know. We have many additional international responsibilities around the world, far more than we can back up with our military forces available, in my opinion. We're over-extended very badly, and this has been recognized by the president in the so-called Nixon Doctrine.

I think this pretty well winds up the Bureau of Ordnance phase of my career. The Secretary and my fellow bureau chiefs gave me a very nice party when I left, a very fine testimonial. It was a very interesting and demanding and productive period of my life, from the Bureau of Ordnance I was returned to sea and went to Japan as commander of U.S. Naval Forces, Japan.

Q: Was this something you sought?

Adm. W.: No, Admiral Burke made the assignment. He called me one day on the telephone to tell me about it. The position involved living in a very beautiful half-Oriental, half-Western Japanese house in Yokuska, in the town, outside of the large naval base which was being operated then and still is being largely operated by the U.S. Navy, with increasing participation by the so-called Japanese maritime self-defense forces, the postwar navy of Japan. Really, the position had become by the time I assumed it with the rank of rear admiral - my predecessors had all had the rank of vice admiral - it involved essentially no command of operating the naval forces, except airplanes. It was more or less a glorified naval district command in a foreign country, and, as such, had many interesting complexities and challenges.

Initially, it happened that the so-called Commander, U.S. Naval Forces Korea - U.S. Naval Forces, Korea - was ill and not functioning, so I made one or two trips to Korea, notably to their naval academy at Pusan. This also was an interesting and challenging experience.

Withington #3 - 179

The command in Japan included the several activities on the island of Okinawa. It included a large air base at Atsugi, and another one at Iwakuni, in western Honshu. There were one or two ammunition depots and large communications facilities at Kamiseya, and another large naval base on the southern island Kyushu, at Sasebo.

I assumed the command on the 1st of April 1958 and was relieved three years later on the same date in 1961, having finished exactly three years, two years plus a one-year extension. Admiral Burke very kindly allowed me to go home with my wife for a month's leave, so that we had this respite in between the second and third year, I was able to hitch a ride home with the Secretary of the Navy and to get back with a minimum of personal expenditure.

Q: Who was SecNav at that time?

Adm. W.: Mr. Franke.

Communication with the Japanese at the highest military levels was relatively simple because the officers in high command generally spoke fairly good English. My wife attempted to learn to speak Japanese and, in fact, at the end of three years was able to converse with Japanese ladies, which had been her motivation. I did not have the time to study the language itself, but I studied hard the pronounciation of the language so that with the help of our interpreter on the base at Yokosuka and the aid of recordings which he made and which I followed, I was able to make speeches in Japanese intelligible to the Japanese. The pronunciation of the language is logical and much simpler than the pronunciation of English.

Q: The pronunciation is almost phonetic, isn't it?

Adm. W.: It's always the same. "I" is always "e," for instance. In every polysyllabic word, the stress is the same on every syllable. It was very interesting.

Q: That must have been a somewhat impressive thing to the Japanese

Adm. W.: They appreciated the effort very much. It was amazing to read the words which I knew, in general, the import of, since I'd written this little speech in English I knew the general import but not specifically what the words meant, to look into the eyes of my audience and see comprehension. I'm still amazed by this experience.

Q: Did you have to make many speeches in Japan?

Adm. W.: Quite a few, yes. There is a Black Ship Festival at Shimoda. This was the color of Perry's ships in the 1850s. There' a monument there, and all the units of the Seventh Fleet parade, and it's rather heart-warming, the ceremony at the Perry monument, the speeches, etc., and games around the hotel in the evening in which we all participated, and the ambassador always made a point of going. The ambassador in my time was Douglas MacArthur, the general's nephew.

Q: The mere fact that he bore the MacArthur name cranked him in, did it not?

Adm. W.: He was a very effective ambassador. I had occasion to work closely with him, and to become good friends with him, and his wife with my wife. During this period from 1958 to 1961, his major achievement - or contribution, I should probably say - was to re-negotiate the security treaty with the Japanese, which was then up for re-negotiation after the initial peace settlement which was completed under Secretary Acheson nine years before.

I might finish up this business about the Japanese speeches. At the end I was asked to go several places and plant a tree, among them the defense academy which is close to Yokosuka on the shore of lower Tokyo Bay. I had the same little tree speech prepared in Japanese, so I was too lazy to rewrite it and I delivered the same speech about four times, and the local Japanese district commandant had to smile and listen to it four separate times as if he was still enjoying it, which I seriously doubt!

Q: Tell me, is one a public figure in Japan, American or otherwise, plagued by reporters in the same sense that he is here?

Adm. W.: There was one very unfortunate press conference. Out at Iwakuni we were running airplane flights in the Sea of Japan, which were doing snooping. The planes were elderly and flyable, but not much more than flyable. One of them was attacked by a North Korean jet, MIG, and hit but not shot down. The tail gunner was wounded and there was bullet damage in some of the hydraulic systems in the airplane. The plane was flown by splendid airmanship to a little used Japanese field on the Sea of Japan, in the west - not a U.S. field. Subsequent to this unhappy event, the crew was brought to Yokosuka for a press conference, and in the press conference the young pilot mistakenly gave the impression that the plane had not had adequate spare parts for the machine guns. This word hit the fan in Washington and Congress immediately and justifiably was up in arms because they had in fact provided ample funds for maintenance of the aircraft machine guns of the Navy. There was an official investigation of this event, and eventually it died out for lack of further public interest. I think Congress forgave Admiral Burke, and Admiral Burke forgave me!

The young tailgunner was brought to the Yokosuka hospital to recuperate and he was put on the television, and a picutre of the press conference was in one of those editions of *Life* of the day. This was a very unhappy event actually and in the public relation angle, both.

Another public relations story of possible interest - Senator Hugh Scott was a naval reserve officer, and he came out as a captain for training duty with the Seventh Fleet. This was approximately 1960. At the end of his tour he was to be flown in to the air base which was manned by the Marines at Iwakani. The so-called COD plane that carried him - onboard delivery plane - lost first one radio set and then the other, so they had no communications at all. They ran into very thick weather and couldn't find Iwakuni, so the pilot in the soup headed generally east, looking for some place where he might come down. He eventually landed safely in a dry stream bed on the island of Shikoku, south of Hon. By great ingenuity, the Marines and the Navy together were able later on to fly that plane out by the use of Marston matting.

Well, for hours we didn't know where the senator was or whether he was alive or dead, and Withington was sweating copiously. When this happened, the local farmers with the speed of light almost got the word around to the local governor that the dignitary had landed unexpectedly. He was given a feast and a Japanese style bath and was generally made the hero of the occasion, which he was, of course.

When I saw the senator at Yokosuka the next day, I apologized for our Navy's inability to get him a safe airplane ride. He forgave me. I have since seen him in Washington and he repeated his forgiveness! So we almost lost a United States senator, and this was not good.

Q: Tell me about the tie-in with the Seventh Fleet command. How did that tie in with your over-all naval command?

Adm. W.: We, of course, were responsible for the naval facility at Yokosuka, which repaired the Seventh Fleet ships and other Navy ships, and a similar repair facility at Sasebo. We had a large intelligence outfit on the staff whose chief function was to collect intelligence for the operating forces, not only in the Seventh Fleet and Western Pacific, but the whole Pacific Fleet. And we did the best we could to support the Seventh Fleet in every possible way. This involved also, when appropriate, the use of my public relations officer and his staff. My role was at that time entirely in support of the forces afloat, and I recognized it as such and tried to be of maximum use to the Seventh Fleet commander.

Q: On the average, how many naval ships were repaired or serviced in a given year at these Japanese bases?

Adm. W.: Enough so that there was great concern by the shipyard people on the mainland. This was cheaper to do in Japan than it was in our shipyards, either government or private. So that there was constant pressure, particularly from the political angle, to reduce the amount of work in Japan, and there was a very tenuous balance between what could be done economically and what could be achieved politically.

Q: Send the ships home for more expensive repair!

Adm. W.: That's right. This was higher than my level, but I was quite aware of what was going on, of course. Incidentally, there were two very fine airplane re-work facilities in Japan also, which were much cheaper than those on the West Coast of the United States and there were similar political difficulties about using them. We did use them, however, and saved the Navy money.

Q: Tell me about the attitude of the Japanese people and the Japanese government in this time. Your period there covered the time when General Eisenhower was going out and had to cancel.

Adm. W.: Yes, and there was a riot at Haneda airport and the presidential secretary and the ambassador were inside a car and barely got out after the student rioters had beaten on the top of the car with whatever they had in their hands.

Q: Did you, as commander of the naval forces, have repercussions?

Adm. W.: There was a very interesting incident at this time. Every June there is a Queen's Birthday celebration at all the British embassies all around the world, and it happened that this was exactly the time for the Queen's Birthday reception in Tokyo. I consulted with the ambassador who was not going to go to the Queen's Birthday reception. My superior, militarily, was the Air Force general command, and he wasn't going to go. So I decided, by golly, somebody better wave the flag for the Queen, and I went with my wife. We got through with no great difficulty, although some of the hired demonstrators were in the streets, and we had to take evasive action a couple of times. I happened to be the senior U. S. officer, military or civilian, present, and did my best to represent the United States, and I'm still glad that we did this. The ambassador later thanked me for going.

Q: He didn't go because of the ...

Adm. W.: He had Mr. Hagerty, the presidential secretary, with him, and he didn't want to go out in the streets until things had calmed down a little bit. I didn't blame him.

Q: Were these demonstrations aimed entirely at United States representatives, or did they also involve British and others?

Adm. W.: No, it was entirely against the United States. There was, and is still, a strong element of the radical left in Japan, which says that the security treaty with the United States should be junked. They don't say how they propose to defend Japan if anything happens, because the self-defense forces are totally inadequate to do this, and the Japanese government knows it. They have a free security ticket through the security treaty and we, in effect, defend their country. Since we also suffer a trade disadvantage with them currently, things are getting rather uncomfortable and ticklish in both directions. In my time, 1958 to 1961, the trade balance was much more equitable. In fact, it was largely in our favor, and this indirectly paid for the cost of the U. S. forces which were deployed in Japan.

Q: In your time, the tremendous boom in Japanese enterprise in exports and so forth was only just beginning, was it not?

Adm. W.: Yes, but it was quite clear that they were on their way. Already the air in Tokyo Bay on the western side, which was our side, was blackened with smoke from the steel foundries between Yokohama and Tokyo. The smog was already well started. The energy of the individual Japanese was clearly apparent. They under-live us and out-work us, and they still do that. This is one of the reasons they're going to continue to prosper, in my opinion. As you know, their gross national product has been increasing in recent years at a ten percent or higher rate. I don't see how this can be sustained very much longer, and if it should drop even to a five percent rate for Japan it will be a major depression. But the frightening ability of the Japanese to under-live and out-work the occidental is a fact which makes me have nightmares every once in a while.

Q: What is your prognosis about this? Will the Japanese, like the Americans before them and apparently as the Russians now, want more material things, material comforts of the world?

Adm. W.: This is already happening. Japanese production of automobiles is astoundingly high. As you know, they are extending more and more their sales in the United States, but are also obviously selling most of their products within Japan, and people are able to buy. The standard of living of the Japanese is risin

The apartment house is a phenomenon of recent years, and has freed the Japanese housewife. When she lived in a little wooden house with Shoji screens and no locks she could never leave the house safely. Now she can lock the door to her aparto, no matter how small it is, and go off and play with her friends in the afternoon or do anything she pleases. And she has, generally speaking, the service of an automatic electric rice-cooker, which is big enough to handle the family's ration for the day. She just leaves it plugged in and forgets it, and it never burns, and it's always ready. We brought one from Japan home with us.

The social structure of Japan has altered greatly. In the old days, papa never carried a baby or had anything to do with it, or with the care of children. Now, you'll see occasionally fathers wheeling babies in their carriage, which are something new in Japan, and something they can afford to have.

Q: Well, as the standard of living rises in Japan, will there not be some equalization of prices in terms of exports and imports?

Adm. W.: I don't know how the export-import system will go, but certainly a larger fraction of the national output will go to the people and to the consumer product industry. You asked about the attitude in Japan toward the United States. It was amazingly friendly. I don't know whether this is still true in Japan or not. We have visited the country once since retirement and found it to be so. We in my time, of course, after the security treaty had been signed were there by invitation and not as conquerors, and the invitation apparently was sincere.

We occasionally met a Japanese who hated all Americans because of the defeat in World War II, but these were mostly old and bitter men. This did not include Admiral Nomura, who was the ambassador in Washington at the time of Pearl Harbor. I mentioned earlier having sought him out.

Q: Yes, you did. You said that the Japanese government was well aware of their inability to defend the country, and aware of the fact that they were depending on the U. S. shield for its defense ...

Adm. W.: They didn't want to spend their own money, and they don't today.

Q: But are they not inhibited in moving in this direction becaus of the attitude of the people who have been surfeited with war?

Adm. W.: Yes, and also the constitution is very specific that Japan shall never, repeat never, maintain military forces. So that actually and honestly to develop a modern army, navy, and ai force it would be necessary for the Japanese to modify their constitution, which was imposed upon them by the occupation forces under General MacArthur. Politically this would be very difficul if not impossible, to do. So they just pretend that the self-defense forces are not an army or navy or air force, but they really are. It's very difficult and very oriental.

Also, as a matter of interest, there is not a secretary of defense, There is a director general of the defense agency who i not on the same level as the secretary for foreign affairs, for instance, or the secretary of the treasury. Actually, of course, is a powerful man because he spends a lot of the government's money. But this money has never and to this day, I think, has never reached, let alone exceeded, one percent of the gross national product. It's a very small investment in their security which they make for themselves and only possible because of their security treaty with us.

Q: But do you see an end to our protection in the near future?

Adm. W.: I don't feel competent with my crystal ball to make any prediction. There seems to be a growing realization among responsible people in Japan that there is nothing inherently evil in nuclear weapons. Politically, I think that it's very doubtful that they will, within the next ten years at least, have any nuclear weapons of their own. There's a very delicate business about whether or not any nuclear weapons should be left on the island of Okinawa after the Japanese take it over. I don't know how this is going to turn out. I don't know what was agreed upon in private behind the written words of the treaty which has now been approved by the Japanese and which will shortly be sent to the Senate.

Q: Do you anticipate any change in Japanese attitude once the Chinese government begins to get a great deal stronger on the mainland? I mean in terms of military effectiveness?

Adm. W.: The Japanese have a basic regard for the Chinese, knowing that historically their civilization came from China many, many hundreds of years ago. They have two religions, the Buddhist, which came from India via China, and the Shinto, which is local

Withington # 3 - 1

nature-worship. Culturally, their architecture derives from China, notably the Ise shrine, but is now very much Japanese. The old buildings at the Ise shrine are rebuilt, as I recall every five to ten years exactly as they were before, so as to be sure that everything is exactly alike and nothing is ever going to fall down. Some of the wooden buildings, which are still the type of architecture throughout Japan, and always in the temples, have survived since 600 and 700. You can see them still in the old capital at Nara, near Kyoto.

Q: You said that since the commander in South Korea was ill you had seen those units as well ...

Adm. W.: Just for a brief period, yes.

Q: At Pusan ...

Adm. W.: We went to Seoul, also.

Q: And this proved to be a challenge. Would you elaborate on th

Adm. W.: Yes. I had to attend the graduation at the Korean Nava Academy and make a few suitable remarks. How I was supposed to d this, not knowing much of anything about Korean, was somewhat dif ficult to figure out. I forget now what I said, I'm pretty sure it wasn't very adequate, but at least I responded when called upo Since I had to speak in English, and these boys didn't have much English, although they had some which was in their course, I'm afraid the effectiveness was very reduced.

This was a very interesting new adventure. The families wer there to watch their sons graduate, and back in the audience they were sitting there, the old men with their conical hats and the Korean robes, and the mothers and grandmothers in the typical Korean dress, whose name I forget now, but it's well known and not at all similar to the Japanese native dress.

As I think I mentioned before, it was at this time in Seoul that I arranged to call on President Syngman Rhee. This was not too long before the end of his career. My call consisted primarily of listening to him talk which was most interesting and lasted some fifteen or twenty minutes.

Q: His English was...

Adm. W.: His English was superb, of course, yes. He had been for years a Protestant minister - I think a Baptist minister - in the Hawaiian Islands before he returned to Korea after World War II.

Q: And he was in exile for a certain period of time in the United States.

Adm. W.: Yes, that's right.

Q: You said that your command also had to deal with Okinawa and several of the islands there. Would you talk about that?

Adm. W.: We had a naval air station down there, quite separate from the big Air Force base complex at Kadina. We also had a communications station. The Third Marine Division headquarters and many of the men were on the island and they received support from me, primarily through the large exercise area on the slopes of Mount Fujiyama. They would send men up from Okinawa and train ashore. This was a very politically delicate matter. The farmers didn't like to have the Marines there, but they didn't like either to think of their not coming because the money being spent in the area wouldn't be spent any more. This was a matter of political concern during my whole three years in Japan. I was interested to note several years ago that we were forced to give up this very large maneuver area, which was too bad because there was never enough real estate on the island of Okinawa for large military maneuvers, and after all the Third Marine Division deployed something on the order of 15,000 officers and men.

Q: But when they came up to Fujiyama they were curtailing some of the agricultural production?

Adm. W.: No. This was largely a desolate lava-strewn area, but the farmers, as a matter of principle, didn't like having people around, except they liked their money. We managed somehow to fulfill the request of the Marines for use of the area while I was present in Japan, with some considerable difficulty. As I say, later on, for political reasons, we had to give up the use of the area.

We did a great deal of traveling in Japan, to Nagasaki two or three times. At that time we paid for two destroyers out of U.S. funds called "Offshore Procurement," and we went to Nagasaki first for the launching and then later for the commissioning of the destroyer <u>Akizuke</u>. Mrs. Withington was the sponsor, and this involved not a bottle of champagne but a bottle of sake, and it involved a fearful and wonderful Rube Goldberg device with a platform on the speaker's stand, a rope across the platform, and a hatchet. Mrs. Withington's job was to cut the rope with the hatchet in one blow. The night before the launching our host arrived in our hotel with a mock-up of this stand and a piece of rope and a hatchet, and gave her a dress rehearsal.

Well, the bright day dawned for the ship launching, and when the time came, the cue was given, Mrs. Withington raised the hatchet, not in one hand but in both hands, protruded her New England jaw to the maximum degree, let fly like Carry Nation, and with the first blow severed the rope. Once the rope had been severed, the trigger for the launching was hit, the ship started to move, the saké bottle at the end of a long rope swung and hit the bow and broke into a thousand pieces, a large ball at the bow of the ship broke and out came pigeons and balloons. Everybody cried!

Q: Everybody cried?

Adm. W.: Yes, everybody cried. It was very moving.

Q: Why was Nagasaki selected as the place for that?

Adm. W.: The Mitsubishi shipyards are there. Now I believe, in fact I know, that the supertankers, these 200,000-300,000 ton behemoths, are being made in Tokyo Bay, Sasebo, and also on the inland sea, I believe at Kure. I don't think that they can be gotten out of Nagasaki Harbor that size. So I suspect that the shipyard is somewhat reduced in its importance to what it was in my day.

Q: In Nagasaki did you visit hospitals and so forth?

Adm. W.: We went once from Iwakuni to Hiroshima and visited the hospital and saw some of the human remnants of the bombing. We then, and I believe still, maintain the medical mission which followed the victims of the bombing at Nagasaki and Hiroshima, that furnishes what help can be given and studies the genetic effects of the first nuclear bomb blast on these poor people.

Q: How did you find their attitude toward you? As an American representative?

Adm. W.: They were more kindly than I would have expected, but it was an obvious strain on both sides. I would not like to repeat the experience. There is a memorial at "the ground zero point" at Hiroshima where I laid a wreath. The hostility during this little event was quite obvious. I was glad to leave. It was curiou[s]. The attitude in Hiroshima was definitely hostile. The attitude in Nagasaki, which had been similarly bombed and grievously hurt, was not hostile. I don't understand this. I didn't understand it then and I don't now.

Q: Is there any correlation with the state of recovery?

Adm. W.: No. Nagasaki has always been a seaport. It was in the days the country was closed, and the Dutch had a concession on a little island in the harbor. Hiroshima was and is, I think, a manufacturing town but not a major one. I don't know why this should be. But it's true, and, as you know, I think since the war ended Hiroshima has been the center in all of Japan for anti-war groups. Why this should be rather than Nagasaki, I have no idea. Except, for one thing, it's on the main island and Nagasaki is tucked away on the south island, pretty well south, on Kyushu.

Q: Did you get up into the northern regions?

Adm. W.: We visited Hokkaido once in summer and had a very interest[ing] and pleasant adventure. There was then - I don't know whether there is now or not - a small communications activity in connection with a military airfield. I'm of the impression that the Japanese have now taken over this airfield completely.

I went up there more or less as an excuse to visit the island, and I also wanted to indicate some interest and support for the young officers and the men who were detailed up there.

Q: Was that airfield there anywhere near the Sea of Okhotsk?

Adm. W.: It was close to the strait between Hokkaido and Honshu.

The influence of the Americans in the northern island is quite apparent, both in the cities which are laid out in our style with many brick buildings, and on the farms which have many brick farm houses. It's really astounding. It looked almost like Montana in this hilly country. There are a great many livestock, including horses, raised on the island. Incidentally, the Japanese are very fond of horseracing and, as you know, baseball is the national pastime. This continued to be true even at the height of World War II.

I wouldn't like to predict, and won't, what the long-range outcome of our relationship with Japan might be. Up to now, it's surprisingly good. The current trade disagreement is not minor, it's major. It may have very unhappy effects. But it is not true, as Admiral Nomura once remarked to me, that the interests of Japan will always be parallel and essentially similar to those of the United States. They will always be looking out for their own interests, and I hope that we'll continue to look out for our own the best we can. I would hope that, generally speaking, in the Western Pacific, our interests and theirs would remain parallel, particularly as regards basic relationships with China, and by "China," I mean Communist China.

Q: They still have the same problem of over-population which they had prior to World War II, don't they?

Adm. W.: Oh, no. The Japanese have controlled their population. They are now essentially stationary at about 100 million. There are over a million legal abortions a year. They're also using the famed pill...

Q: How many legal abortions?

Adm. W.: Over a million legal abortions a year. They're using all of the birth control methods known to the West also.

Q: Even 100 million is too much for the Japanese islands, isn't it?

Adm. W.: It's too much unless they're able to continue their present ability to import raw material and export finished goods. This is the way they've done it. They are now self-supporting in rice, which is astounding because only 15 percent of the country is arable. Their industry and their ability to get things done is literally astounding.

Q: Is there any obvious fear of Russia, especially in Hokkaido?

Adm. W.: I think the Japanese are very uneasy about the Russians, yes. There is a group of, I think, three small islands north of

Hokkaido which are of no importance whatever to Russia, but which Russia refuses to return to Japan, and this is a very sore point between the two countries and will continue to be so.

Q: In your time you spoke of having considerable intelligence teams under your command, obviously watching the China situation...

Adm. W.: Yes, and the Russian...

Q: Has that been curbed since then?

Adm. W.: I really don't know. It was a rather expensive investment in manpower and equipment in my day. Whether this has continued I can't say. The information, presumably is just as important now as it was considered to be then.

Q: Did you get to Taiwan at all? Did your command have anything to do with Taiwan?

Adm. W.: My classmate Admiral Smoot was in charge in Taiwan for a long time, and we visited the Smoots down there for a short period. We did not meet the Generalissimo, but we met the head of the armed services and were feted for a period of a couple of days. The only support I had to give Taiwan was very curious in a way. Admiral Smoot was a good man with his hands and his tools in making furniture, and this interested Madame Chiang Kai-shek. One day I got an urgent message from Smoot to Withington: Madame wants a small lathe, such and such a type. That's all he said - as soon as possible. Well, I knew who Madame was without any further decoding, so I sent for my aide and he searched the area. I think he had to go to Tokyo before he found this thing, and we got it off in a plane to Taiwan within twenty-four hours! This was my only urgent item of support during my three years for Taiwan.

Q: Did this indicate the fact that the Madame also had an ability in this area?

Adm. W.: That I can't say. She had developed an interest through becoming aware of Roland Smoot's work with his hands and tools. She's a very interesting and formidable woman. We visited by air once the other commands in the area, which were at Guam and the Philippines and Taiwan, and this was an interesting and profitable experience for us.

Q: I know the commander of the Seventh Fleet has numerous social functions which are also quasi-diplomatic, and I would assume that a large portion of your duties based on the main Japanese islands were also of this nature?

Adm. W.: Our social schedule was very heavy. We had a very considerable staff at the quarters - a driver and servants, including two Japanese Navy widows who were more or less the sparkplugs of the whole staff and who had been there since immediately postwar. Two fine women.

Q: They knew the protocol.

Adm. W.: They knew what was right, especially what should be done in large dinner parties which we gave often in honor of visiting dignitaries, usually American. We had a dining room which, at a pinch, could seat twenty-four, and these large dinners were pulled off with great aplomb by our staff and we came to look forward to them very much. It was a fine way to meet Japanese people. For instance, one evening the mayor of Yokohama came to dinner. He came in a kimono. He knew nothing about the use of Western eating tools, so we provided him with hashi, or chopsticks, which he used with great skill.

Q: But he had to be seated at a table?

Adm. W.: Oh, yes, of course, and he indicated his appreciation of the food by smacking his lips loudly and belching, which is a very, very polite thing to do in Japan, and which astounded the young woman alongside of him who hadn't been in Japan more than a few days! She didn't quite understand such behaviour.

I remember those dinners well. I think we did some good with them.

Q: I hope you had an adequate expense account to cover these!

Adm. W.: Yes, I did. The money came from CinCPacFlet in Honolulu. I don't know whether this is still true or not. This covered the cost of the liquor, the wines, and in general the food for the official entertainment.

Q: What sort of an official dwelling did you have?

Adm. W.: I mentioned that it was an old half-Western style, half-Japanese style, the Japanese commandant's house which was built about 1910. It was designed as a matter of fact by BAron Uriu, a graduate of the Naval Academy class of 1888.

Q: Admiral, you returned to the United States in 1961, and retirement came shortly thereafter, did it?

Adm. W.: Yes, the 1st of April, 1961.

Q: Since you were a man of considerable vigor, what did you do with your time, your leisure then?

Adm. W.: I didn't have to work for financial reasons, and I was available and called upon by the Navy for several boards and advisory boards. One of these was a board to review the Navy's training program. In 1961 I joined the advisory board of the Naval Ordnance Test Center at China Lake in California, and spent five years there. Later, I was on the advisory board of the Naval Propellant Plant at Indian Head, Maryland, the advisory council of the Naval Weapons Laboratory at Dahlgren, and lastly - I've just left this one - the ordnance advisory committee under the Naval Research Advisory Council, which was concerned with the work at NWL, Dahlgren, and NOL, White Oak.

Q: Would you mind taking these various boards one at a time and giving me a little idea of what they accomplished in your time?

Adm. W.: It's very difficult to say what an advisory board ever accomplishes. We used to talk about this among ourselves. The membership of the boards slowly rotated, of course. They would be mostly distinguished civilian scientists and engineers. We wondered among ourselves whether we really ever did any good or not, and we arrived at a consensus, I think, that the answer was, "yes," that for the preparation for the board meetings it was necessary for the station to make a running estimate of the current situation so they could tell us what was going on. And, incidentally, find out themselves. In a place as big as Naval Ordnance Test Center this takes some doing. It's enormous. In this sense, the reviews were very useful to the station and, I think, to the Bureau of Ordnance.

The Naval Ordnance Test Station at China Lake involves a large air facility and much airplane flying. It has since been taken over first by the Bureau of Naval Weapons, and now the Naval Air Systems Command. It's no longer part of the Ordnance Command.

At Indian Head the main effort was not making gunpowder any more, although the facilities are still there, but making propellant grains for rockets. They had this work to do both for the Navy and for the Army and Air Force. It was important when the expenditure of ammunition of this type for Southeast Asia was very large. It was important also, of course, during the Korean War.

Dahlgren has developed from being a proving ground for guns primarily to a very much broader-based laboratory with some of the finest computer facilities and personnel in the world.

I was also asked on an ad hoc basis to be on the visiting committee of the postgraduate school at Monterey in 1966, which I thoroughly enjoyed, being of course an alumnus years back myself, when the school was at the Naval Academy. I participated in two reviews of the guided-missile program for the Bureau of Ordnance - the Bureau of Naval Weapons, I should say. Admiral Stroop was the first head of the Bureau of Naval Weapons, and on his own initiative called upon me and the former chief of the Bureau of Aeronautics, Admiral Pride, to review his actions in the Bureau and give him a frank opinion of what was good and what was bad about the outfit. This was a very honest and commendable action on his part, and we did our honest best to tell him what we thought. I hope our report was useful.

Q: That certainly would be a constructive effort.

Adm. W.: Yes. The marriage between ordnance and aeronautics was just then, under the Bureau of Weapons, beginning to become effective and, unfortunately in my opinion, before many more years passed there was another reorganization of the Navy Department and the two activites were again divorced. I thought then, and still think, that this divorce was a great error.

Q: It's very upsetting, is it not, to the ongoing function of a bureau ...?

Adm. W.: Yes, you're right, and the senior civilian people are disturbed in their work when they're reorganized. They're still the same people, but with different boxes round their names, and I think there's entirely too much fiddling with the organization of the Department of Defense and the Navy Department in recent years, entirely too much fiddling.

Q: Why is this? Because of the fact of the union of the services under the Department of Defense?

Adm. W.: One reason I think is pressure from the Secretary of Defense to modify our organizations within the Navy to be more similar to those of the Army and the Air Force, which are basically similar to each other. I think the Navy has been at fault in havi

Withington # 3 - 203

so many reorganizations. An ambitious Secretary of the Navy gets into office and wants to do something, so he changes things around.

Q: So very often a secretary of the Navy is not deeply immersed in naval affairs, is he?

Adm. W.: No. How can he be? So he has to depend on his advisers, and they have personal axes to grind, maybe. In some cases, I'm sure they did.

Q: You skipped over the one that had to do with training.

Adm. W.: This was also under Admiral Pride, as a matter of fact. There was concern that there were too many individual activities within the Navy concerned with training, which had always been basically the responsibility of the Bureau of Naval Personnel. We talked to everybody. We even went out to the Special Devices Center on Long Island which, among other things, produced the so-called Link trainer, the stationary cockpit which was a mock-up of the actual airplane, which is now used extensively by all air forces and also civilian aviation in the early stages of training pilots in a new type of airplane.

As a result of our report, if my memory is now correct, and it's not necessarily so, a director of naval training with considerably more power than any individual then had was set up in the Navy Department, I think in Op-03. I believe he's still there. But the whole thing was more or less vitiated because we weren't allowed to consider naval air training, and this was sort of illogical, you see. Recently all naval training has been centralized under one commander.

Withington #3 - 204

Q: What was the board that you just stepped down from?

Adm. W.: The Ordnance Advisory Committee, which was concerned with ordnance matters at the Naval Ordnance Laboratory at Dahlgren and the Naval Ordnance Laboratory at White Oak.

Q: Well, Admiral, hearing you review your service on these various boards and ad hoc committees puts one in mind of the original intention of the General Board, as it existed in the Navy some years ago. Using the abilities and wisdom of retired senior officers or senior officers who are approaching retirement for the general advantage of the Navy. This is a more flexible system now employed, I take it?

Adm. W.: Yes, I would say so. Admiral Jim Russell has similarly served on a good many boards for various purposes. So has Admiral Sides, and so have others. Admiral Stroop, I know, has been or still is a member of the advisory committee at the Naval Ordnance Test Station. It's a good way, I think, to utilize the experience of retired flag officers.

Q: You in retirement from the Navy have not served on industrial boards?

Adm. W.: I am currently a member of the board of managers of the Navy Relief Society. This is an activity very dear to my heart. The board meets once a month, and I'm also a member of the finance committee and of the pension trust committee and executive committee. So that I'm involved more or less on a continuing basis with matters concerning the Navy Relief Society. They have currently some

1,200 children of officers and petty officers, and Marine officers and petty officers in college on interest-free loans, and the amount of money involved has grown to be something in excess of three million dollars. After a rather slow start because of inadequate publicity, this activity is now well known and for loans up to $1,200 to as many as 500 or 600 children a year gets up into pretty large numbers. So far, the repayment experience has been exceedingly good. Far better than 90 percent, I think it's 95 percent. This might not continue. Of course, the tying-up of all this capital without interest is a contribution that the Society makes to the children. I think it's a very fine effort.

Q: There's no tie-in with a retirement home like Vinson Hall and Navy Relief, is there?

Adm. W.: No. We made a loan of two million dollars that made the construction possible, and made it at the low rate of 5 percent. The Vinson Hall activity is still a struggle. They don't have enough apartments rented to carry the operating expenses and pay off their loans. The Federal National Mortgage outfit, Fanny Mae, which now has a new name guaranteed the our-two-million-dollar loan, so even if Vinson Hall regrettably should fail or renege, the Society would not be out the two million dollars.

Well, I should say in conclusion, looking back on my life in the Navy, I don't regret a minute of it. I regret my mistakes. If I had it to do over again I would certainly try to do better, and I would like to have a chance.

Q: Thank you very much, Admiral.

INDEX

for the

Series of Interviews with

Rear Admiral Frederic Stanton Withington,

U. S. Navy (Retired)

AEC (Atomic Energy Commission): 107, 110; university laboratories under contract to, 111

AKIZUKE, Japanese DD: financed by the U.S., 193

Amphibious Group Commander: Withington (Nov. 1952-Dec. 1953) becomes commander of Group 3, 119 ff; in Korean waters, 126; exercise at Camp Pendleton, 126-127; simulated use of atomic bomb, 127-128

Anderson, RADM 'Squeaky,' USNR: beachmaster at Eniwetok, and other pacific islands, 71

Applied Physics Laboratory, Silver Spring, Md.: 146-147; summary of work on missiles, 147-148; longevity of missile programs, 148-149

Armed Forces Special Weapons Project: 106

Atsugi, Japan: American Air Base, 179

Bausch and Lomb: 33

Baxter, Dr. James Phinney: lectures at the National War College, 103

Belgian Congo: province of Katanga, source of uranium supplies, 114-115

Bennett, Dr. Ralph (Captain - USNR): 83-84, 86

Berkeley, 2

Blandy, Adm. Wm. Henry P.: buys Swedish AA guns to meet U. S. needs as WW II approaches, 44; establishes an R and D divison in BuOrd, 45

Briscoe, RADM Robert R.: in command of OpDevFor, 93, 97, 124, 126

Bryant, VADM Eliot H.: Division commander in Mediterranean, 97

Bureau of the Budget: control over expenditures in BuOrd, 172-173; press conference in Detroit with comments on role of

Bureau of Budget, 173

BU ORD (Bureau of Ordnance): duty with Bureau immediately following graduation, 16-17; fire control desk in 1939, 44; R and D becomes important, 45; early use of radar, 46; limited supply of machine gun ammo at time of Pearl Harbor, 47; rush orders for ordnance immediately after Pearl Harbor, 48, 50-51; discussion of build-up of Ordnance before WW II, 49; problems related to speed-up of building program, 51; manner of dealing with allotments to foreign countries, 52; circumventing legal requirements, 53; strain of first few months of WW II, 56; assigned to BuOrd, Nov. 1944, 79-80; fire control unit, 80; concern with post-war termination of contracts, 80-81; succeeds upon death of Admiral Parsons as Deputy in BuOrd, Dec. 1953, 131; rivalry between BuOrd and BuAir, 133-134; duties as Deputy, 136-137; responsibility of Bureau Chief for Congressional relations, 137-138; comments on solid propellant rockets vs liquid fueled, 144-145; status of things when Withington took over as Chief of Bureau in 1955, 150-151; discussion of development of Polaris program, 151-160; annual preparation of the budget, 165-166; comments on Ordnance and new ship design, 167-168; increasing complexity and cost of ordnance, 169; research and perfectionism in the military, 170; activities of Bureau of Budget inside BuOrd, 172-173; press conference on Budget, 173; criticizes rising weapons cost, 174-175; closing of Naval Gun Factory, 176-177

Burke, Admiral Arleigh: 153; 178-179; 182

USS CAMBRIA: Headquarters ship for Adm. Hill and amphibious force, 66; 79

Campbell, General Levin - Gold Medal: awarded to Adm. Withington by American Ordnance Association (1958), 174

Chiang Kai-chek, Madame: 197

USS CHICAGO, CA: on Alaskan cruise, 39

Cluverius, ADM Wat Tyler: serves as Captain of BB WEST VIRGINIA, 19-20

USS COLUMBIA, CA: 61

Control Instrument Co.: 48

Cowdrey, RADM Roy Thomas: 58

Dahlgren assignment, 26-27; dive bombing experiments, 29

DASA - Armed Forces Special Weapons Project: responsible for Sandia Base School, 135

Dean, Gordon Evans: head of AEC, 110

Demobilization: comments on hasty action, 81

Des Moines, Iowa: 1-2

DEW (Distant Early Warning) Line Operation: 119-120; Canadian cooperation, 121; blackout of communications, 121-122

Dowell, The Hon. Cassius C., Member of Congress: 3

Draper, Dr. Stark: Professor at M.I.T., 45

Einstein, Professor Albert: consultant to BuOrd, 45

Engebi: Adm. Hill decides to enter atoll at Eniwetok before making attack which came first on islet of Engebi, 68

Eniwetok: Adm. Spruance decides to send reserves under Adm. Hill to take island, 67-68; campaign makes reputation of Adm. Hill, 70-71; comments on thermonuclear explosion there, 118-119

USS ESTES: command ship for DEW line expedition, 122

Fiji Islands: 61

Fire Control, in ships: 162; summary of development of modern systems of fire control, 162-164

Ford Instrument Co.: 33; manufactures Mark I, AA computer, 44, 48, 164

Forrestal, The Hon. James: Secretary of Defense, attended R and D meetings, 166

Foster, The Hon. John S., Jr.: Head of R and D in Pentagon, 140

Franke, The Hon. William B.: 173, 179

Freeman, Dr. Douglas: historian lectures at the National War College, 103

Gates, The Hon. Thomas: Secretary of the Navy and later Secretary of Defense, 157-158

General Electric Co.: 48

Gleason, Miss Louise: future Mrs. Withington, 23; comments on marriage in 1926, 23

Guam: assault on island led by Admiral Conolly, 78

Hanafee, Comdr. Frank Joseph: 55

Hayward, VADM John T. (Chick): incident during flight with Admiral Sherman, 135

Hewitt, ADM Kent: 35-36

Hill, Admiral Harry: 65 ff; Withington becomes his chief of staff 65; headquarters ship the CAMBRIA, 66; description of Admiral Hill, 67; Pacific reputation made with Eniwetok campaign, 70-71; uses serves of Squeaky Anderson as beachmaster, 71; sends Withington home on mission to Washington, 71; engages in preparations for Saipan, 72-73; President of National War College, 100, 103, 105

Hill, VADM Thomas B.: heads office of Naval Atomic Energy, 109-110

Hiroshima, Japan: visit to hospital there, 193; hostility towards U. S. in the city, 194

Hooper, VADM Edwin B.: 135; heads research division in BuOrd, 136

Hoover, The Hon. Herbert - former President of U. S.: delivers lecture at National War College, 103

Hussey, VADM George: 80, 82-83

USS INDIANA, BB: 22, 25; Capt. Merrill as skipper, 56; problems of shakedown cruise, 57; armament, 57-58; radar equipment, 58; damage control, 59; spare parts, 59; complement, 60; in South Pacific, WW II, 61-63; operation off Gilbert Islands, 64; Withington detached to become Chief of Staff to Adm. Harry Hill, 65; Capt. Fechteler also detached same date, 65

Industrial War College: 103-104

Intelligence: value of for island hopping, 69-70

Inyokern: Naval Ordnance Test Center (Nots) at China Lake, 138-139, 142; 145; Withington in 1961 becomes member of Advisory Board, 200; 201

Ise Shrine: personifies Japan's cultural debt to China, 190

Iwakuni, Japan: American Air Base, 179; intelligence missions flown from over Sea of Japan, 181

Japanese Naval development: remarks on progress made by Japanese in decade of 1930s, 36-37; comments on U. S. progress in same period, 36-37; 38

Japanese People: demonstrations against U. S., 185; their enterprise, 186; standard of living, 187; constitutional prohibition against military forces, 188; birth control, 196;

fear of Russians, 196-197

Japanese Propaganda: 72-73

Johns Hopkins University: operates Applied Physics Lab at Silver Spring, 146; 148-149

JUPITER Missile: Army project, 154

King, Fleet Admiral E. J.: 47, 55

Kwajalein: amphibious landing on, 67-68

Korean Naval Academy: visit at time of graduation, 190

Korean War: 123-124

Lauritson, Dr. Charles: Professor at CalTech, develops air-to-air rocket, 145; member of Board of Advisors at NOTS, 146

Lee, VADM Willis A., Jr.: 95

Lockheed Mfg. Co.: 157-158, 169

Long Beach, Calif. earthquake: 34

LUCKY BAG: 2, 8-9

MacArthur, The Hon. Douglas, III, U. S. Ambassador to Japan: 180 difficulties with Japanese demonstrators, 184-185

Majuro: amphibious landing on, 67

USS MANCHESTER, CL: Withington in command for period of Mediterranean cruise, 1948, 97

MANHATTAN Project: 159

Mark I Rangekeeper: early fire control computer, 162-163

USS MARYLAND, BB: used for bombardment in Pacific, 64-65

USS MASSACHUSETTS, BB: failure of 16-inch shells to explode, 63

McNamara, The Hon. Robert: Secretary of Defense, 140, 142; comments on fixed price-contract basis, 170

Merrill, VADM A. S.: 56-57

Military Liaison Committee: connecting link between AEC and military, 107

USS MISSISSIPPI, BB: United of OpDevFor, Withington in command, 92; complement, 96-97

Montgomery, Capt. Robert, USNR: 61

Nagasaki, Japan: launching ceremony for U. S. financed destroyer - AKIZUKE - with Mrs. Withington as sponsor, 192-193; lack of hostility among people, 194

National War College: Withington named to class of 1949; discussion of lectures, courses, etc., 100-105

Naval Academy Experiences: 4-5, 7-11; aviation requirements, 12; comments on curriculum and teaching methods, 13-14; discipline, 14-16

Naval Atomic Energy Office: 106-119; Withington to #2 job under Admiral Tom B. Hill, 106; takes orientation course at Sandia, 106; 1951 succeeds Adm. Hill, 109; immediate concerns, 109; general comments on weapons testing, 111-112; efforts to develop breeder reactor, 112; missile warheads, 113; discussion of raw material sources, 114-115; reasons for lessening security in atomic matters, 115-116; extent of knowledge about nuclear matters in navy, 117; Withington attempts to teach brief course on atomic energy for benefit of naval officers, 117; Eniwetok tests, 118; naval unit at Kirkland Field, 135

Naval bombardment: comments on skill of old BBs in Pacific campaign, 70-71

Naval Gun Factory: 32-33; closing of Gun Factory, 176-177

Naval Ordnance: comments on lack of progress in 1930s, 37-38; secrecy concerning warhead exploder in torpedoes did not permit use at sea, 41; failure to equip DDs with A.A. guns,

NOL (Naval Ordnance Laboratory): Adm. Hussey assigned Withington as Director - Oct. 1945, 82; scope of assignment, 83; personnel, 85; acquires Kochel wind tunnel from Germany, 86; German scientists, 87-88; comments on employment of scientists in government work, 88-91; experience aids him in development of rapport with scientific and engineering men, 167

Naval Ordnance Test Center (NOTS) -- see *Inyokern*

Naval Propellant Plant, Indian Head, Md.: Withington becomes member of Advisory Board, 200-201

Navy Relief Society: 204; Withington a member of Board of Managers, 204; Society loans two million for construction of Vinson Hall, 205

Naval Research Advisory Council: Withington member of Advisory Committee, 200

Naval Research Laboratory: beginnings of the Lab, 45

Naval Research Office: cooperation with BuOrd, 166-167

NAVAL REVIEW: edition of May, 1970 with account of POLARIS program, 151

Naval Secrets: comments on stultifying measures, 41-42

NTDS (Naval Tactical Data System): 163

Naval War College: turns attention in 1930s to possible conflict with Japan, 40; Withington assigned for special course after amphibious command in Pacific, 130

Naval Weapons Lab. at Dahlgren, Va.: Withington becomes member
of advisory council, 200-201

NEVADA, BB: 21, 30, 34

Nimitz, Fleet Admiral C. W.: minute awareness of battle actions
on Saipan and Tinian, 79

Nomura, Admiral Kichisaburo (Japanese): 124-125; 195

Norden Bomb Sight: 42

Norris, John G.: Reporter on Washington Post for scientific
matters, 174; article on retirement speech of Withington,
174-175; 176

USCG NORTHWIND: icebreaker, on DEW line expedition, 122; comments
on Russian ice breakers, 123

NOTS: see Inyokern

Noumea: base for BB INDIANA in South Pacific, 62-63

Okinawa: U. S. naval facilities on island, 191; problem of
Marines training in Japan, on slopes of Fujiyama, 191

OpDevFor: 54; testing of 5-inch batteries in fleet, 93; use of
old battleships for conducting tests, 94; scope of interests
of this program, 94; origins of concept, 94

Oppenheimer, Dr. Robert: 90, 110; 128-129; 131

Panama Canal: war games include surprise air attack on Canal, 32

Parry Island: third in Eniwetok group to be occupied by U. S.
Forces, 69

Parsons, RADM Wm. S. (Deke): death of (Dec. 1953) results in Adm.
Withington being assigned as Deputy Chief of BuOrd, 130-131;
his support of Sidewinder missile, 138-140

Pearl Harbor Naval Base: state of things before WW II, 39-40;
amphibious exercise off Oahu, 41

Philco Corporation: 143

USS PITTSBURGH, on European Station: 22

Point Barrow, Alaska: 120

POLARIS: missile test, 129; 151-160; non-secret nature of program contrasted with MANHATTAN project, 159; 170-171

Post Graduate School: 26; visits to Ordnance Installations, 26; comments on P.S. course, today, 28; Withington serves on visiting committee for Monterey P.G. school in 1966, 201

Pride, Admiral Mel: Chief of BuAir, 201; concern with naval training in all its aspects, 203

Pye, VADM Wm. S.: skipper of BB NEVADA, 30

Queen's Birthday Reception, Tokyo, Japan: 184-185

Raborn, VADM Wm. F., Jr.: 154-158; 170

Radar: comments on pre-World War II radar, 46

REGULUS I and II: first of missiles to be developed, 149-150

Reserve Officers: comments on in World War II, 60-61; material specialists and reservists vs line officers, 53-55

Rhee, President Syngman of Korea: 191

Rickover, VADM Hyman George: 109-110, 152

Rivero, Admiral Horacio, Jr.: number 2 in fire control section of BuOrd, 46

Roosevelt, President F. D.: dispute with Admiral Taussig, 35-36

Ruddock, VADM Theodore Davis, Jr.: gunnery officer in BB NEVADA,

Ryan, RADM Thomas John, Jr.: recommends Withington to Admiral Hill, 66-67

Saipan: preparation for campaign made in Hawaii, 72-75; explosion on LST at Pearl Harbor limits amount of artillery available for operation, 74-75; summary of action, 74-75; attitude of civilians and military towards possible capture, 75-76; conflict between services - removal of Gen. Smith, 76; comments on Spruance efforts to protect onshore marines from Japanese fleet units, 78-79

Sandia Base School: comments on cram course for senior officers, 135

Sasebo, Japan: 179; repair facilities for the 7th fleet, 183

Schuyler, RADM Garret L.: first EDO, 37-38; 44

Scott, The Hon. Hugh, U. S. Senator (Captain USNR): 1960 training duty with 7th Fleet, 182; plane downed in bad weather, 182-183

Sharp, ADM U. S. Grant: skipper of DD damaged in bombardment of Noumea, 63

Sheppard, The Hon. Harry, Member of Congress: 49-50; 141

Sherman, Adm. Forrest: in command of 6th fleet, 1948, 97; CNO, 135

Shimoda: Black Ship Festival in commemoration of Admiral Perry's visit, 180

Ships Characteristics Board: 160; process of designing ships by committee, 160-161

Shoeffel, RADM M. F.: Chief of BuOrd, 133; 165

Sides, Adm. John Harold: missile czar in CNO before Adm. Raborn, 154

SIDEWINDER Missile: Adm. Parsons insists on development, 138-140, 142; Withington concerned that two bids of equal nature be submitted, 143-144; 145; BuAir accepts the SIDEWINDER, 143; 146; 150

Sixth Fleet: mission in Mediterranean, 98; occasional trips to Black Sea, 98-99; bases on Riviera, 99

Smith, Prof. C. Alphonso: 9

Smith, Gen. (Howling Mad) Holland: 77

Smoot, VADM Roland: 197

USS SOUTH DAKOTA, BB: 61

Spiderhole battle technique: employed by Japanese on Eniwetok, 69

Spruance, Adm. Raymond: despatches force to take Eniwetok, 67-68; removes Gen. Smith on Saipan, 76-77; comments in approval of Spruance decision not to draw naval forces from vicinity of Saipan while operation continued on land, 78-79

Strauss, RADM Lewis L.: served in BuOrd at outbreak of W.W. II, 46, 47, 110

Stroop, VADM Paul D.: succeeds Withington as Chief of BuOrd (1958), 174; as first head of Naval Weapons, called on Withington and Admiral Pride to review his actions, 201-202

STYX Missile System: present development of Russians, 149

Taiwan: visit to island, 197

TALOS Missile: developed under contract with Convair and Bendix, 147-148

Tarawa: 64-65

Taussig, VADM Joseph K.: Withington becomes his Flag Lieutenant, 34-35; remains a RADM because of earlier disagreement with FDR, 35-36; 38

Teller, Dr. Edward: 90

Tinian: Adm. Hill placed in command of assault, 77; details, 78

Turner, Adm. R. Kelly: Commander of Saipan operation, 73; orders

Withington to prepare plan for administration of Saipan, 73-74; 78

Tuve, Dr. Merle Antony: 88, 146-147

Underwater Demolition Teams: comments on their effectiveness in Pacific campaign, 77

U. S. Naval Forces, Japan: Withington named Commander of, 1958-1961, 178 ff; functions temporarily as Commander, U. S. Naval Forces, Korea, 178; comments on Japanese protests against visit of President Eisenhower, 184-185; social functions as part of assignment, 198-199

Vinson, The Hon. Carl: Member of Congress, 50

Vinson-Trammell Act: 49

WEST VIRGINIA, BB: assignment to new BB, 17-18; deck duty and staff communicator, 19-20, 22; runs aground on her initial cruise, 22-23; lack of damage control in ship, 24; gunnery capabilities, 25; 60; in Australia, 31

White Oaks, Maryland: location of NOL, 83-84

Wigglesworth, The Hon. Richard, Member of Congress: his knowledge of naval ordnance, 141; 166

USS WINSLOW, DD: lacks AA guns, 43

Withington, RADM Frederic Stanton: early background data, 1-2; initial interest in Naval Academy, 2, 4; forebears, 5; comments on early marriage for midshipmen, 18-19; family statistics, 30; develops ulcer while serving as Chief of Bureau of Ordnance, 56; comments on his own naval career and value of sea duty, 132-133; retirement, April 1, 1961, 200

Yokuska, Japan: headquarters for Commander, U. S. Naval Forces,

Japan, 178-179; ability of Withington with Japanese language 179; 181; repair facilities for 7th U. S. Fleet, 183; comments on policy of repairing U. S. ships in Japanese ports, 183-184

www.ingramcontent.com/pod-product-compliance
Lightning Source LLC
Chambersburg PA
CBHW080614170426
43209CB00007B/1425